Over the Sea from Skye

by

Ian G. Macdonald

Grosvenor House
Publishing Limited

Ian G. Macdonald is hereby identified as author of this
work in accordance with Section 77 of the Copyright, Designs
and Patents Act 1988

The book cover picture is copyright to Ian G. Macdonald

This book is published by
Grosvenor House Publishing Ltd
28-30 High Street, Guildford, Surrey, GU1 3EL.
www.grosvenorhousepublishing.co.uk

A CIP record for this book
is available from the British Library

ISBN 978-1-78148-516-3

Over the Sea from Skye

To Prince Edward Island

.....

(The intriguing tale of Murdoch and Effy MacLeod)

In memory of
My dear brother
Duncan
(1940 – 2010)

Chapters

.

Acknowledgments

The publication of an historical book requires much more than the author's input; others make important contributions, either wittingly or unwittingly. The characters, of course, had no option, they lived their lives, had their good times and bad times, and left their mark.

I have many people to thank for their help in the production of this book; firstly, Ms. Joanne Lea and Matthew Hatvany for their discovery of the 4 letters, and Ms. Catriona Parsons for her translation of letter 1. Dr. Angus MacDonald first set the ball rolling by suggesting that I might be interested in investigating further, and the readers of my two previous publications encouraged me to attempt another book concerning *An Tir, an Canan, s'na Daoine* (the Land, the Language and the People) of our beloved Island of Skye.

Along the way I had considerable assistance from Angus MacLeod (Brue, Lewis) and his enormous files of Skye families, Anne MacLeod and Alison Beaton at the Portree Archive Centre, as well as from Margaret MacDonald and her staff at the Clan Donald Centre (Museum of the Isles). Much of the historical background was gleaned from the volumes listed in the bibliography at the conclusion of this book, but several other individuals had a significant input, namely; Charles MacLeod (Arnish, Raasay and Bayfield, Portree), Donald MacDonald (Aros Portree), Rebecca MacKay (Raasay), George Sanborn (PEI) and members of the Portree Local History Society.

Jan Norris from Braintree, MA, USA, a great-granddaughter of John MacLennan Lot 67 PEI, formerly of Raasay, mentioned in Chapter 10 of the text, was of considerable assistance, as were Fred and Diane Vickerson and Anna-Lee Hogan of Charlottetown PEI, but the largest contribution undoubtedly came from Brian Cox, my other e-mail correspondent from the 'far side of the pond'. His vast database of information on the pioneers of the Scotch Settlement on Prince Edward Island, and his access to relevant maps, helped me to discover much more about the fortunes of Murdoch and Effy MacLeod and their family.

Many thanks go to my brother Sorley and my sister, Christine Thomson for their proof-reading and encouragement, and to my wife for her continuing forbearance, tolerance and patience.

Any remaining errors or misinterpretations are my own.

Ian G. Macdonald

The Emigrant's Prayer

Oh, Jesus Saviour, when we part,
Obedient to thy will,
From friends and home with sinking heart,
Do Thou be near us still.

Go with us Lord; our vessel guide
Across the pathless sea;
And grant, what'er we leave behind,
We never part from Thee.

Oh, go with us! Appoint our lot,
And lead us on our way –
Companion in the loneliest spot,
Light in the darkest day.

Go with us Lord; our labour bless,
Our "basket and our store";
And o'er the distant wilderness
The streams of mercy pour.

If clothed and fed, and sheltered there,
We rich abundance find,
Oh let us not withhold a share
From those we leave behind.

And grant, when'er our voyage cease,
Wher'er our home we raise,
That home may be a home of peace,
A home of prayer and praise.

Peace through the Saviour's cleansing Blood,
The Holy Spirit's aid;
And praises to the Triune God
In grateful homage paid.

Foreword

In the year 2000, while having a chat about ancestry and the former inhabitants of the Braes district of Skye, where we both live, my local G.P. at the Portree Medical Practice, Dr. Angus MacDonald, eldest of the famous Glenuig Pipers, mentioned that he had come across four interesting letters from the 19th Century, relating to the Braes township of Camustianavaig.

Dr. Angus, who formerly had worked as a family doctor in Cape Breton, Canada, had been reading a copy of the *'Abegweit Review'* (Volume 8, Number 2). He was sure I would be interested in the contents and promised to get me a copy. True to his word, he presented me with the material some days later.

I was intrigued, inspired and hooked! Could I possibly find out more about these interesting people? Did they keep up their Gaelic language in their new homes? Belonging, as I do, to a Presbyterian background myself, I was also interested in how the emigrants continued this tradition in Prince Edward Island. But first I needed to learn more about the 19th century conditions in my great-grandparents' home township.

As I was then very busy with my duties as Depute Head Teacher at Portree High School, I could not see my way to following up all the connections suggested by reading the letters, but promised myself, God willing, that I would get round to this at a later date.

In 2006 I took early retirement after 33 years in the teaching profession, and commenced catching up on the many projects I had filed away. On behalf of the Aros Organisation, I began conducting cultural tours for visitors around Skye's 'Trotter-nish Wing' and researching the History, Natural History, Mythology and Folklore of that area. This resulted in my publishing *'Like a Bird on the Wing'* in early 2008. Much encouraged by the success of that book, and the demand from friends to continue researching material from the rest of the island, I published *'On Wings of Skye'* eighteen months later. Only now, in 2010, have I got round to following up the inter-esting tale of Murdoch and Effy MacLeod of Camustianavaig.

This effort is not intended to be an academic work, but rather, I hope, a blend of genealogy, history and enquiry.

In order for the reader to begin where I began, please now go ahead and read the four letters.

Ian G. Macdonald

CHAPTER 1

Letters from Camustianavaig

"'N' uiseag air a sgiath,	"Skylark on the wing,
Seinn gun fhiamh a ciùil,	Sings it's uninhibited song,
'S an ceò mu cheann Beinn Tìonabhaig,	The head-mist on Ben Tianavaig,
Is an sliabh fo dhriùchd."	And the moor bedecked with dew."

Mairi Mhor nan Oran

Letter 1

Effy MacDonald to Murdoch MacLeod
(see appendix 1 for original)

[Envelope]
    Mr Murdoch MacLeod
    Squire Wright
    Prince Town Road
    16 miles from Charlotte Town
    Prince Edward Island
    North America
[postmark May 20 1831]

[The first fragment is missing ....then.....]

.....Iain Campbell: a bed; twenty barrels of seed ....from Beni-filer [Penifiler] they themselves have now sold the place and given it up. I took it before I got your letter and I'm resolved to work the croft. Along with that the autumn was wet, we had a lot of snow and frost over the winter and we're having a wet

1

spring. You'll be planting for us, if you are wanting us after writing this letter. Iain Breabadair (the weaver) from Raasay, was saying in my house that he himself and his sons are with MacKenzie who used to be signing people up. He got 27 families at the first meeting in Raasay. They are going over after May market in 2 ships. Tell what extra trouble there is between getting your letter and our letter. I don't have ___ [time] to put more in it but my thousand ____ [blessings] to yourself, son, and tell will I give more school to go a distance for any sense whatever that is in us. Give our blessings all together to Alasdair and his people and how good they have been to you and Alasdair is useful in sending news.

Norman is sending his kind compliments to you Murdoch and to his sisters and brothers. You yourself know that I was most desirous of going there, if there was not any trade whatsoever going on. I was obliged to get married and there is no regret whatever on me but to be missing my sisters and brothers. I was advised by my mother's brother John Campbell and it was around August Fair I did it. It's from Anna MacLean that I have got three parts of all what he had and half of the boat and nets. Iain Campbell is saying that what I got went for 35 pounds and you tell me or will any other worry come on me which of them is better for me to go or stay with your father and I am putting my ____ it would be worse than going if you consider your father that it would be better for me to go than to stay at the way that I have considering my situation. Write to me as you said since I'm telling you where I am and _____ I expect to build a house and since you _____ on me I won't build it until I get your letter. Anna is sending you her blessings and to all the relations and to your own self Murdoch. Send word to my godfather(?), Roderick, and tell him that his people expect him to send them a letter and I myself would like to get word about him. Your mother is sending blessings with added good wishes to you indeed, and I will be glad to see you, if you wish, and everybody at Alasdair's as well.

Letter 2
Effy MacDonald to Murdoch MacLeod

[Envelope]
   Mr. Murdoch MacLeod, Esq.
   Care of Alex'd [Alexander] Campbell
   Malpeque Road
   Prince Edw Islan
   [post marked Portree, 1832]

Camastianavaig 23rd May 1832

Dear Murdo,

I received your letter and I am very glad to hear you are in good health and prospering so well in the world, and this is to inform you that I am in good health at present, thanks God for it. Hoping this will find you in the same.

I have heard you are going to marry & if you think that expedient and lawful for yourself to do you may do it for I hope I'll never trouble you for it for I have none to take care of in this cause but myself and I hope by God's grace I shall keep myself chaste and virtuous tho you should prove so perfidious as to forget the name of Effy Macdonald and attach yourself to another but if you do that God grant her a better usage than I got and may He never impute to you as a crime my sufferings; at His judgement seat.

You are getting strange news from your Friend, but I think the friend is a good inventor of lies. He told you in his letters that I burnt the letter you sent me from Tobermory, but you need not believe that. It is like every other adious [sic, audacious, odious] news you hear about me and my relatives for I have the letter carefully in my vest as dry as my silk handkerchief. I would not burn a letter from a more inconsiderate person in my esteem than you. I declined sending it in this letter to you for fear of putting you to expenses but I'll send it by some emigrant from this to that Island this year to let you see

3

the malevolence your friend bears to me in giving you such an account of me and my relations. You heard that I did not visit your father while laying sick. By witness of some of my neighbours I was there several times but there were some persons in who would not say a Single word to me since my going in till I went out again tho it was not your father or mother.

They are all now intending to emigrate to that country being prepared for it having roped [sic, rouped] all their goods and furniture and set off the land. You were saying in the late letter you sent me that you would not believe anything I would say in my own justification unless you father was witness of it. Your father is now going and you shall learn of him how things are at present. You were grieved at my sending you an unlocked letter before but you must excuse me it was not my fault for I delivered the unlocked letter to Norman Campbell and he promised me he would lock it. I was newly delivered as I told you and was unable to go anywhere for wafer and wax to lock it. What you shall have [unclear word follows] that what was spoken of my [unclear words] is to write shortly himself and he says he is much obliged to you for letting him know it. But is not my business to the answering for such. You must excuse me for the direction [postal address in PEI] as yourself did not let me know how to direct to you. My compliments to yourself and to my uncle and aunt. My mother and all the family sends their compliments to the same and begs them to write to them as soon as you deliver their compliments and are greatly surprised that they got no news of [them] before this. My compliments to Alex'd [Alexander] Campbell and am much obliged for declaring he would be my friend [sponsor]if I should go there but he has as many thanks as though I would trouble him. I desired the little boy [Murdoch and Effy's son Murdoch (Jr)] to send you his compliments. The boy said he would do it tomorrow & he expects every day to sail in a little boat to see yourself and he'll not bring his grandfather lest he drink too much of the whisky on the way. Norman Campbell does not intend to go at all he is building a new house [and] he

[is] in good health and sending his compliments to his father, stepmother, brothers and sisters.

I am your affectionate Wife
Effy MacDonald

Letter 3

John Campbell to Murdoch MacLeod

[Envelope]
   Mr. Murdo MacLeod

Squire Wright Lot 67 Anderson Road
Scotch Settlement
Prince Edward's Island
North America
[post marked 17 ? 1838]

Camastianavaig, Portree Parish 13 August 1838,
Dear Murdo,

Your letter dated the 16th Dec'r 1837 came to my hands in Spring and I don't doubt you are a little surprised for my being so long silent but you need not, because I was willing that people might evancine [evince?] themselves, and that I would examine then too but that was of no effect. Effy your wife is anxious of reaching you as any wife on earth could be but what can the wishes of a woman do when she has no means to assist her, she has nothing in the world and her father Hugh is the very Hugh you have seen yourself there is no alteration and therefore she is unable to do anything in going where you are unless you do it for yourself. Therefore my opinion and advice to you if you regard your wife or children is to send for them immediately because they are very well worthy of any trouble you can take for them, because the children would be a grace and delight to many a prince in a palace, they are in good health and is present with me this very moment, if you are anxious of getting your wife and children as I take you to be I do not know

5

what will detain you but you must come yourself personally or else send a check on the national bank office at Portree to put money to any friend on whom you would depend to act for you and likewise instructions and directions to her on her arrival what to do and who to find you out the above you must send to me or some other friend and if not, you need not be troubling yourself upon the subject. Minds your son is not in the mean time in but while he was in school he was very good to learn but is not able to sign his name there is no school this side of Portree so as poor people cannot reach at it. You must not be blaming Effy if she was as able to reach you as I understand you are to reach her there is a long time since she had gone. Murdo I was very much surprised that you did not mention any thing concerning that colony and my old acquaintances and especially your father. But although not I shall acquaint you of some of the country news in the first place. I have to let you know that I am in good health but my wife is always poorly. There is a mineral well or fountain found in Stenshal in the Eastside of Trotternish such as that one that is in Dingwall which is of great comfort to many and my wife is there at present. The oldest of my daughters married and is very well off but Marion had the misfortune of losing her husband, and she is married again the second time. Chirsty my youngest by the first wife is likewise on the point of marrying, Jessy the oldest by the second wife is in Portree in the Sewing School and she is a fine girl. Malcolm and Alexander is likewise in Portree School. Malcolm is learning the Latin language since two or three years past and on the three last examinations of the school he has gained the prize and Sandy is getting on very well too and John the youngest boy is in school. I have to let you know that I got a letter from a friend of mine from New South Wales Australia one Charles Campbell to send Malcolm to himself because he has made a fortune there but I think I shall not [unclear line but appears to be "send him there four years"]. You may tell your father and my friend Alex'd Campbell if they have done well for themselves they have done exceedingly for Hugh and his children because they are the only men here now. They built a storehouse and they now fish curens [?] buying herrings and freighting vessels, you can tell your father that Donald Kennedy failed in Upper Ollach and that the farm was offered to me and I refused it and that because I would only get a lace [lease] of five years only, I was afraid if I would be turned out at the end of the five year I would not get as good a chance as what I had. Time would fail me in telling you all I would wish. Peter Beaton and his family is just as you have seen them. Angus Nicholson Drumaoish has four boys and Samuel his brother is lying idle not doing a turn for a long time past, your Uncles daughter and her mother is in the old condition. Kenneth your friend is still a bachelor for this time a twelve month was a very severe time and this summer was so with some too, but we have a fine appearance of crops this year and good price of cattle, but through all the dearth that was in the country I did not buy a grain. I have no more to add, Effy is present during the whole time. I am writing in the hopes of fulfilling of your former promises and matrimony vows to her and the presence of the Almighty God who will judge you and her and the presence of men also joins me with her love and best respects to you.

I am your sincere friend and best wishes.

John Campbell.

PS

I was on the point of forgetting that that I made your certificate publickly known in all companies and places in which I happen to be and likewise thank you for forwarding it. John Campbell.

Letter 4
Effy MacDonald to Murdoch MacLeod

The following is a direct quotation:

[Envelope]:
Mr. Murdoch MacLeod
Prince Edward's Island
Anderson Road Lot 67
North America
[post marked May W 27 N 1839]
Camastianavaig 23rd May 1839

Dear husband

Your welcome letter came to my hands yesterday evening which gave me unspeakable satisfaction to hear of your welfare and the more so for the contents it contained. I have the pleasure of letting you know that I and the children enjoys good health and the boy is continually at school, I was making all the [unclear something like arrangements] that was in my power for emigrating since Martinmass until a letter came to Dugal MacPherson from a relation of his that is married upon Alex'd Campbell's daughter Mary which contained that you sailed for to come here in October last and that discouraged me very much [she was discouraged because he never arrived, and she feared he may have been lost at sea], but now I revive and hope if the Almighty sees it proper to prosper with me I shall embrace the first opportunity of seeing you. There is to my opinion about 200 of the Raasay people for emigrating to that Island and if the Almighty spare me you may depend undoubtly of my being along with them wherever place they [a line is missing here] certain as yet what time because they did not get a vessel yet but they disposed of all there subjects [belongings] and is making ready every day with all the speed they can, some of them were promising to do the best assistance they could with me, but I rather think they have enough to assist themselves.

Arch'bd My brother and Ann my sister both married last winter. Archy and a lad from Flendranes? (unclear) one MacKay bartered the one married the other's sister. Tho as I have the intention of going I will not add any more but conclude with my best respects to you your children is present in the mean time and joins me with the same I remain you ever Loving Wife
Effy MacDonald or MacLeod

CHAPTER 2

Background

In 1974 the four letters above were donated to the Public Archives and Records Office of Prince Edward Island, Canada, by Ms. Joanne Lea, an agent for a philatelist company in London *(located at 1 The Adelphi, John Adams Street, London, England)*. We can only speculate as to how the letters (with envelopes) were removed from Prince Edward Island and came into the possession of the London philatelist company, but the value of the stamps on the letters would seem to explain their interest in them.

The four letters were sent to Murdoch MacLeod, Lot 67, Prince Edward Island (formerly of Camastianavaig, Isle of Skye, Scotland) from Effy MacDonald and John Campbell, Camustianavaig. They span the years 1831 to 1839 and are now preserved in the Public Archives and Records Office of Prince Edward Island *(PARO 2727/1-4)*. Few were aware of their existence (including archival staff) until they were discovered by Matthew Hatvany, while undertaking another research project. The letters are of great interest in regard to Scottish emigration and settlement in P.E.I.

Mr Hatvany has transcribed letters 2, 3 and 4, which were written in English, and, for letter 1, received assistance from Catriona Parsons, Professor of Celtic Studies at St. Francis Xavier University, in translating parts from the original Gaelic. He wishes to make readers aware that obscurities in the original letters, misspellings, lack of punctuation, physical damage and poor photocopies made transcribing the letters a less than definitive process.

The Importance of the Letters

Matthew Hatvany writes in the *'Abegweit Review'* (Volume 8, Number 2).

> *"These letters are of particular interest for the insights they provide into the experience of emigration that many Scottish families underwent in leaving their native country. The letters relate some of the optimism that accompanied emigration to the New World, but more often, the heartache of separation of family members, and the difficulties of those who stayed behind in obtaining accurate knowledge of kinfolk and former neighbours who undertook a passage overseas. They also indicate the choice and strategy that some Scottish families exercised in deciding whether to emigrate, how to do so, and to what place emigration would proceed. Most significantly, the letters illustrate that emigration from Skye was not always a homogeneous affair. The letters relate that some people remained at home because of their individual prosperity, while others were too poor to raise the necessary capital to uproot. Once emigration was decided upon, some families went to North America, while neighbours were drawn to the South Pacific.*
>
> *"The letters are only a small piece of evidence in a much larger story of Scottish emigration during the nineteenth century. Nevertheless, they are a significant and sentimental addition to our understanding of one Highland family's experience in going to Prince Edward Island."*

Having read all of this I was intrigued, and indeed ashamed that I knew so little about conditions in Skye and the causes and pressures for emigration in the early 19th century. Was it indeed poverty? Was it eviction? Were conditions so harsh that it had become too difficult for these people to remain in Skye? Why did they not go to the major Scottish cities to find work? On the other hand, were there times when emigration was seen in a positive light? Were the people motivated to go because of the encouragement of others who had gone before?

I now believe that there were many complex reasons, some positive and some negative, *"the push and pull of emigration"*, which led to what the author Lucille H. Campey, who has studied Scottish Emigration in great detail, calls *"An Unstoppable Force"*.

So what more can we glean from the story of Murdoch and Effy?

Who were they? Who were their relatives? Why did Murdo go? Why did Effy stay? Did Murdo come back for her and/or did Effy go alone? What became of their children? Was there a happy ending?

What of their relatives in Skye – am I one of them? Are there any other connections to present day Skye-folk or modern Prince Edward Islanders?

With some help from publications and archive material available in Skye, in PEI and on the internet, we will try to answer some of these questions in the following chapters.

CHAPTER 3

The Two Islands

First of all we must take stock and compare these two Islands.

Both the natives of Skye and of Prince Edward Island, because of pride in their particular homeland, refer to their local place as *"An t'Eilean"*, "The Island", as if there were no other worth a mention! Is this an inherited characteristic?

Nowadays (2010) both islands are comparable in that they are attached to the mainland by bridges; Skye, across the Kyle of Lochalsh to mainland Scotland and PEI across the Northumberland Strait to New Brunswick.

An t'Eilean Sgiathanach (The Isle of Skye)

"O Eilein mhóir, Eilein mo ghaoil,

Is iomadh oidhche dhiubh a shaoil liom an cuan mór fhéin bhith luasgan

Le do ghaol-sa air a bhuaireadh

Is tu 'nad laighe air an fhairge,

Eòin mhóir sgiamhaich na h-Albann,

Do sgiathan àlainn air an lùbadh

Mu Loch Bhràcadail ioma-chùilteach,

Do sgiathan bòidheach ri muir sleuchdte

Bho 'n Eist Fhiadhaich gu Aird Shléite,

Do sgiathan aoibhneach air an sgaoileadh

Mu Loch Shnigheasort's mu 'n t-saoghal!"

"O Great Island, Island of my love,

Many a night of them I fancied

The great ocean itself restless,

Agitated with love of you

As you lay on the sea,

Great beautiful bird of Scotland,

Your supremely beautiful wings bent

About many-nooked Loch Bracadale,

Your beautiful wings prostrate on the sea

From the Wild Stallion to the Aird of Sleat,

Your joyous wings spread

About Loch Snizort and the world."

Sorley MacLean

The Isle of Skye, situated at 37°N, on Scotland's northwest coast, is the second largest of the Scottish isles and the largest of the Inner Hebrides. It is separated from the mainland of Ross and Cromarty and Inverness-shire by the Kyle of Lochalsh and the Sound of Sleat.

The island is justly renowned for its spectacular and rugged scenery and was perhaps first inhabited by bands of hunter-gatherers in the Mesolithic or Middle Stone Age. These sojourners were succeeded, in due order, by the Picts, the Celts and the Vikings. In modern times, many people from around the world know it as *The Misty Isle, Eilean a Cheo*, but another title, and perhaps an older one (Dean Munro 1549), is *The Winged Isle*.

"The iyle is callit by the Erishe, Ellan Skyane, that is to say in English, the Wingitt ile, by reason it has maney wyngs and points lyand furth frae it thro the devyding of thir lochs."

The first name of this island, noted by the Roman cartographer Ptolemy in his early map, was *Scetis* and the Norse called it *Scaia*. The historian Adamnan, in his *"Life of St Columba"*, writing around 700 AD, refers to Skye as *Sgia*. This could mean either Cloud Island or Island of Wings.

On looking at a map, it appears that Skye is indeed composed of several wings. *Trotternish, Vaternish, Durinish* and *Minginish* were so named by the Norsemen; the *-ish* ending meaning a headland or indeed a wing.

"Skye or Skianath is the greatest of all the Erbudae or West Isles. It lies from South to North 42 miles in length, and 12 miles in breadth, in other parts 8.

"This Isle is blessed with a good and temperate air, which though foggy and the hills often surrounded with mist so that they can scarcely be discerned, yet the summer (by reason of the continual and gentle winds so abating the heat) and the thirstiness of the air with frequent showers, so assuaging the cold in the winter, neither the one nor the other proves injurious to the inhabitants; the summer not smothering, nor the winter consuming them."

Sir Robert Sibbald, circa 1670

The Isle of Skye has inspired many writers of prose and poetry both in English and in Gaelic.

Scotland's most famous Gaelic poet of the 20th Century, the late Dr. Sorley Maclean, describes Skye as the "big bird of

Scotland, spreading its wings around Loch Snizort and around the world".

> *"Do sgiathan aoibhneach air an sgaoileadh*
> *Mu Loch Shnigheasort is mun t-saoghal"*

His reference to *Loch Snizort*, our largest fjord, is obvious to a map-reader, as it is positioned between the 'wings'; but *'spreading around the world'* in this context, refers to the many Skye people who chose, or were forced, to emigrate to all parts of the world due to the economic circumstances of the 19th Century and to the greed of their landlords.

Eilean a' Phrionnsa (Prince Edward Island)

"*O! Eilein chluainteil, chòm-hnard, uaine,*

An oir a' chuain 'nad aonar,

Gur caomh leam tuar do shlios mu'n cuairt

Fo thoradh snuadhar sgaoilte;

Do raointean feòir tha tiorail, òr-bhuidh'

Anns an Òg-mhios fhaoilidh,

'S nan achadh farsuing corca 's eòrna,

Sàr fhonn bhò is chaorach".

"Isle of lush green rolling pastures,

Snugly cradled on the deep;

Fields of waving corn and barley,

Clover lands of kine and sheep,

Lovely Isle in all thy freshness,

More like fairy-land each hue,

Richly smiling in the sunshine,

'Neath a sky of deepest blue".

Written by Rev. Norman MacDonald (formerly of North Uist) on a visit to Prince Edward Island.

Prince Edward Island is located at 46°N in the Gulf of St. Lawrence, west of Cape Breton Island and is separated from Nova Scotia and New Brunswick by the Northumberland Strait.

Its earliest First Nation inhabitants were the Mi'maq or Micmac people who named the island *Epekwitk* or *Abegweit* meaning *"lying down flat"* or *"cradled by the waves"*. They believed that the island was formed when the Great Spirit laid some dark red, crescent-shaped clay on the blue waters.

Jacques Cartier, the Breton master-pilot, commissioned by His Most Christian Majesty, Francis I of France, 'discovered' the island in 1534 and described it as *"the most beautiful stretch of land imaginable, pleasant in odour – cedars, pines, yews, white elms, ash trees, willows and others unknown. Where the land was clear of trees it was good, and abounded in red and white gooseberries, peas, strawberries, raspberries and wild corn, like rye, having almost the appearance of cultivation. The climate was most pleasant and warm. There were doves and pigeons and many other birds."*

It became part of the French colony of Acadia and they named it *Île Saint-Jean*.

Under the terms of the Treaty of Paris in 1763, which settled the Seven Years War, Great Britain was granted control over *St. John's Island*. On November 29th 1798, the British Government, to avoid confusion between the many *St. John's* around Canada's Atlantic coast, granted approval for a name change to *Prince Edward Island*. This new name honoured King George III's 4th son, Prince Edward Augustus, Duke of Kent & Strathearn (1767 – 1820), who was in charge of all British military forces on the continent as Commander-in-Chief, North America. Edward was Queen Victoria's father.

The island's Gaelic name is *Eilean a' Phrionnsa* and the French *Île-du-Prince-Édouard,* but it also has a number of nicknames: *Gem of the Gulf, Garden Province, Spud Island* and *Million Acre Farm* because of its renowned fertility.

Another name frequently given to this, the smallest of Canada's Provinces, is *The Birthplace of Confederation* because it was here, at the capital, Charlottetown in 1864, that the possible confederation of provinces to form a united Canada was first discussed. It is interesting to note that three languages were employed in the discussion; English, French and Scottish Gaelic.

Prince Edward Island was the inspiration for *'Anne of Green Gables'*, set in Victorian times by the author Lucy Maud Montgomery.

Comparisons

Both islands, 21st century popular tourist destinations, are said to have a temperate climate but Prince Edward Island, not having the advantage of the Gulf Stream, suffers much more severe winters. The Cuillin mountains of Skye rise to 1000 metres in height, attracting Atlantic rain showers in the relatively mild prevailing southwest winds, while PEI's highest point is only 152 metres.

The sizes of the islands are very different; PEI, the 104th largest island in the world, has a land area of 5684km^2 and a present-day population density of 23.9/km^2, while Skye is much smaller at 1656km^2 with population density 5.59/km^2. The 2010 Skye population of 10,000 is much less than half of its early 19th century level.

In 1873 Prince Edward Island became the 7th and smallest province of Canada. Skye still awaits such an elevation in status within the United Kingdom!

Throughout the 19th Century these two islands, 4000km (2500miles) apart, on opposite sides of the Atlantic Ocean, were to become inextricably linked by the blood-ties of emigration.

CHAPTER 4

Scottish Emigration to the Americas

"Anns a' gheamhradh neo-chaoin
Thig a' ghaoth le fead ghoineant',
'S bidh cruaidh ghaoir feadh nan
craobh,
'S iad fo shraonadh na doininn.
Bidh sneachd trom air gach
gleann,
'S cathadh teann mu gach dorus;
Ach bidh lon againn 's blaths,
'S bidh sinn manranach, sona".

"In the surly winter the wind comes with its shrill whistle, and there's a loud moaning among the trees under the blast of the storm. There's deep snow in each valley and heavy drifts around every door; but we have food and warmth, and we're companionable and contented".

Rev. Duncan Black Blair

We read that a settlement of Highland Scots was first made in the Carolinas around 1739. After the failure of the 1745 Rebellion, the clan system began a rapid decline, fanning the sparks of emigration into a flame. 54 ships full of emigrants, from the Western Highlands and Islands sailed for North Carolina between April and July, 1770. The great MacDonald emigration began in 1772 and continued until the outbreak of the Revolutionary War in 1776. In his *"Journal of a Tour to the Western Isles of Scotland"*, in 1773 with Samuel Johnson, James Boswell speaks of the eager enthusiasm of the people, tacksmen and tenants, to migrate to the American Colonies.

Dr MacCulloch in his *"Misty Isle of Skye"* says of these early sailings from the island: *"Emigration had then the glamour of a new idea, and was palatable when the people resorted to it of their own free will. An emigrant ship would call into one of the lochs by night, and, the next morning, a whole township would be tenantless, its inhabitants having embarked to seek fortune beyond the seas in lands where they should only 'again in dreams behold the Hebrides'."*

In 1773, the famous *'Hector'* carried 190 Highlanders to mainland Nova Scotia (New Scotland). These were the first emigrants to go directly there from Britain, but they discovered that about 8000 New England colonists had already preceded them, at government expense, between 1759 and 1762.

Up to 1790 no emigrant from Skye had gone anywhere else but to North Carolina.

'The Polly'

Perhaps the first recorded connection between Skye and Prince Edward Island is to be found in an advert placed in *'The Glasgow Courier'* of 5th April 1803 which reads:-

> *"Wanted: A vessel to carry 400 passengers from Portrie in the Isle of Sky, to St John's or Pictou, Nova Scotia, to be ready for sea by the first of June. The owner of the vessel to be at the expense of fitting up berths, furnishing water-casks and water with fuel and cooking places. The berths for each person to be 6ft by 18in, with the allowance of 56 gallons water and 2 barrels bulk stowage for each person besides sufficient room to be left in the hold for provisions".*

The advert had been placed by an agent for Thomas Douglas, the fifth Earl of Selkirk, philanthropist and colonizer (June

20th, 1771 – April 8th, 1820), and was answered by Thomas Darby the owner and master of *'The Polly'*.

Possible Polly look-a-like

Although many Scots had already ventured to Prince Edward Island before 1803, we know of no Skye natives who had come there. According to *beul-aithris*, however (the tradition of the elders or history passed down to us from our forebears), we understand that some Raasay men had arrived earlier, probably migrating north from the Carolinas. It is said to have been a native of the Isle of Raasay (according to historian Rebecca MacKay) who rowed Angus MacAulay ashore at Orwell Cove! At any rate, Lord Selkirk records that he was aided ashore by; *"Four fine Ross-shire lads – MacRaes. Hauling the boat thro' the mud in true clannish style – I had been talking my best Gaelic, and divided my dinner with them, which seemed to have won their hearts."*

In 1767, Captain Samuel Holland of the Royal Navy had divided Prince Edward Island into 3 counties (Kings County, Queens County and Prince County with the royalties of George-town, Charlottetown and Princetown), 15 parishes and 67 lots.

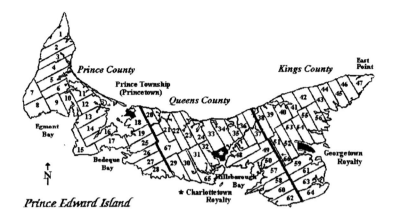

Each lot averaged 20,000 acres and Holland auctioned them off to friends and supporters of the king, with the agreement that these individuals would recruit settlers of British descent to develop and populate the island. Most proprietors signally failed to meet their obligations or indeed, to make any payments, so progress with regard to settlement was slow, but eventually the island began to attract *"adventurous upper-class families looking for elegance on the sea. Prince Edward Island became a fashionable retreat for the British nobility"*.

By the late 1770s, however, 49 of the 67 lots still had no British settlers and 23 of these were completely uninhabited. Like the situation in many parts of the world to this day, the proprietors were sitting back, patiently waiting for the value of their lands to increase. Those settlers who had arrived early, were granted tenancies by the feudal landlords, but were charged high rentals. Highland Scots, used to a similar rack-rental system at home, were among the first to come.

The *'Royal Gazette and Miscellany'* of the Island of St. John (P.E.I.) records the following on 29 July 1791:

"It is with singular pleasure we announce the arrival of those honest and worthy Caledonian emigrants, in health and spirits, notwithstanding a very tedious passage of many weeks. There is not a doubt but that they will receive a kind reception, and

experience that hospitality which so characteristically and eminently distinguishes the Highland race."

Of course, as we have said, many Skye families had emigrated west before 1803, but all had been attracted to North Carolina where the MacDonald Clan had purchased 100,000 acres of good land for the cadets and tacksmen of the clan.

In 1802, John Campbell, the Edinburgh solicitor for Clan Donald, composed a list of tenants of Lord MacDonald who were to be given lands and were now *"going to emigrate to America"* having sold their goods and stock in the Isle of Skye. All the heads of families named in this list are recorded as settled in Belfast, Prince Edward Island, in 1811. They had come there as passengers on *'The Polly'*.

These Skye folk had been influenced to avoid the new United States and to settle in a loyalist area by Dr. Angus MacAulay, a Gaelic-speaking Highlander, who had been a former factor of Lord MacDonald's Skye and Uist Estates. He was the agent, well-placed to recruit the best potential settlers to suit Lord Selkirk's enterprising plans.

As might be expected, of the 800 potential pioneers, the vast majority were drawn from lands belonging to Lord MacDonald, namely Trotternish, the eastern seaboard of Skye, and the whole of South Uist. Added to these were a few families from the neighbouring Island of Raasay and the mainland of Wester Ross.

As MacAulay planned to settle in P.E.I. himself and was married to the daughter of the tacksman of Sartle, Skye, he was in a position to provide information, negotiate terms, allay fears and encourage his fellow emigrants. He commanded the respect of the people and acted as surgeon, schoolmaster and preacher. Dr. MacAulay was later to be elected to the Prince Edward Island House of Assembly and to become Speaker of the House in 1818.

CHAPTER 5

The Old Order

"One of the great advantages of life in the Highlands and Islands in the old days was that the various orders of society were more fully represented in a resident community: the natural leaders of the people lived among them".

Commission to inquire into the Conditions of the Crofters and Cotters in the Highlands and Islands of Scotland — 1884.

The Highland Clan System was one in which the 'children', *(clann)* were loyal to their 'father', the chief. This loyalty was reciprocal and, in turn, the chief gave much needed protection to his people. For hundreds of years, the two main Skye clans, MacLeod and MacDonald, were sworn enemies and fought each other, for territorial advantage, on land and sea, and so raids on each other's clan lands were expected, and elicited a quick response. The chiefs were autocratic and had power of life and death over their clansmen. This authority passed from father to the eldest legitimate son, often arousing jealousies and intrigue among the younger and illegitimate progeny. Second and third sons were usually encouraged to go into the church or the military. In order to occupy the cadets of the clan, avoid internecine conflict, and be in a position to protect the territory from enemies, the close relatives of the chief were granted tacks of land for agricultural purposes. Along with the land, these tacksmen were feudal superiors to the small farm communes already on the ground. The tacksmen were required to provide a levy of soldiers, from amongst their farm tenants, to defend the clan lands or to rally to the chief's flag if he was determined to wage war. The tenants also provided labour for the tacksman's acres, as the professions of stocksmen and tillers of the soil were despised by close relatives of a chief. The system worked to the advantage of all, so long as there was co-opera-tion on both sides. In one account of conditions in 1577, we find that; *"Slait (Sleat) could raise 700 men and Trotternish 500"* for Clan MacDonald; and on the 20 tacks of Waternish, MacLeod of Lewis could muster a force of 200 able-bodied men.

At the beginning of the seventeenth century there was a particularly protracted and bloody war between Skye's two main clans; *'Cogadh na Caille Caime'* (the War of the One-eyed Woman) and Sir Robert Gordon reported that *"their peoples were reduced to such dire extremities that they were forced to eat horses, dogs, cats and filthy vermin in order to sustain life"*. But the final battle in this conflict at *'Coire na Creiche'* (Corry of Plunder), in the Cuillin mountains, finally brought clan warfare to an end.

In 1601 King James VI of Scotland had had enough of their uncivilised ways and warned these chiefs to cease from raiding each other's territories. By 1609 the clan chiefs had signed the *'Statutes of Iona'* which promised their good behaviour, toward each other, and His Majesty's Realm. King James, now James I of Britain, following the Union of the Crowns of Scotland and England, made *Rory Mor*, chief of the MacLeods of Harris (based at Dunvegan Castle), a knight, and granted land char-ters to *Donald Gorm Mor* chief of Clan Donald. This was his method of *"taming the wild blood of the isles"* and it succeeded! In 1616, the chiefs were forced to give further guarantees which gradually began to bring the Old Order to an end. All children, above the age of nine, of the chief men, were to be educated in the south and were to learn English; *"that they be better prepared to reduce their country to godliness, obedience and civility"*. The future behaviour of their cadets was to be the chief's responsi-bility, and these gentlemen were to cultivate home farms and *"be exercised, and aschew idleness"*. Succeeding chiefs of both the MacDonalds and MacLeods were no longer seen as the 'fathers of the clan', but increasingly saw themselves as members of the aristocracy with whom they had associated and been educated in the schools of England and Lowland Scotland. Clan chiefs began to marry 'money' in the south and to employ 'bean counters' to manage their affairs on the territories to which they had increasingly become absentee landlords. The Old Order was gone and the ordinary people were now required to abide by the foibles of the chief's Estate Factor, who might, or might not, be particularly interested in their welfare and affairs, but was employed to make the estate a financial success, in order to pay for the extravagant excesses of the distant proprietor. The chiefs, as individuals, had removed themselves from the clan culture but were still revered, for their office, by their loyal people.

It was Norman ('The General'), 23rd Chief of the MacLeods of Harris who, very tellingly, said of his own class: - They are *"sucked into the vortex of the nation and lured to the capitals, they degenerate from patriarchs and chieftains to landlords; and they become as anxious for the increasing of rents as the new-made lairds, the novi homines, the mercantile purchasers of the lowlands."*

Dr Johnson also made the observation. *"Their chiefs being now deprived of their jurisdiction have already lost much of their influence, and as they gradually degenerate from patriarchal rulers to rapacious landlords, they divest themselves of the little that remains."*

The tacksmen were first to be informed that they were an unnecessary burden on the estate, unless they could pay more into the chief's coffers. They had little option but to increase the rents of their inferiors. Poverty began to grip! Thomas Pennant's comments on the situation were very apt:

> *"Many of the greater tacksmen were of the same blood with their chieftains; they were attached to them by the ties of consanguinity as well as affection: they felt from them the first act of oppression, as Caesar did the wound from his beloved Brutus."*

Skye's trade in black cattle, tentatively begun around 1502, by *Domhull Mac Iain 'ic Sheumais*, gained prominence through the 17th century and continued to provide a very important business, for some enterprising tacksmen, but prices were liable to fluctuate wildly and, in the early days, the roads south were dangerous, due to the frequent activities of highwaymen.

About the end of the 18th century a new industry brought prosperity to those and such as those in Skye! Kelp, tawny seaweed, found in abundance on the sea coast, is rich in alkali, iodine and other minerals. When the weed is cut, gathered, dried and burned, the resulting alkaline ash was used for bleaching linen. As the linen industry was Scotland's most valuable in the 18th century, this discovery was very important. Calcined kelp produced alginates which were used in soap making and for certain processes in the glass industry. Enormous quantities of wet weed were required to make a very little alginate (twenty tons of weed for one ton of ash). Being very labour intensive, many kelpers were required to cut and haul, to stack the wet weed on kilns of smouldering peat, and to rake and bag the resulting ash. The small wage had become increasingly necessary to help pay the rents for the newly established crofts. The alternative to kelp was a substance called barilla, which was only obtainable from Spain. As a result of the Napoleonic Wars, the import of cheap barilla was subject to much difficulty and heavy government duty, and so the price of kelp rose from £1/ton to £22/ton. Kelpers' wages did not! Estate Factors began to encourage kelpers to abandon the communal farms, move nearer to their work at the coast, and to become direct crofting tenants of the estate. Emigration was increasingly seen as a viable option for many redundant tacksmen, but the Factors, for the present, needed their tenants.

In the wake of the abortive 1745 Rebellion, although the MacDonald and MacLeod chiefs had not openly supported the Stewart cause, many Skye and Raasay people suffered fearfully at the hands of the Duke of Cumberland's troops. These were not happy times for the tenants on the Skye Estates of MacLeod and MacDonald, but worse was to follow when the kelp industry failed and the proprietors sought to make a fortune from the wool of the *'caoraich mhor'* the big sheep.

One thing which has changed little over the years for Skye's farming community is the influence of the weather! In 1976 James Hunter was commentating;

> *"… nowhere in the region is the crofter's lot an easy one. The most fertile croft cannot escape the frequent rain and gales that are a consequence of the north-west Highlands' proximity to the Atlantic depressions that track incessantly north-eastwards between Scotland and Iceland; and of all the numerous uncertainties of the crofter's condition, therefore none is more permanent than the weather."*

CHAPTER 6

The 'Polly' Settlers and Settlements

"Perhaps there is no race of people better adapted to the climate of North America than that of the Highlands of Scotland. The habits, employments, and customs of the Highlander seem to fit him for the American forest, which he penetrates without feeling the gloom and melancholy experienced by those who have been brought up in towns and amidst the fertile fields of highly cultivated districts. Scotch emigrants are hardy, industrious, and cheerful, and experience has fully proved that no people meet the first difficulties of settling wild lands with greater patience and fortitude."

1843, Geologist, Dr Gesner, who explored widely in Nova Scotia and New Brunswick.

"..a race of men and women of unconquerable will and indomitable spirit, inured to hardship and unspoiled by luxury".
Malcolm A. MacQueen

There were very few politicians who understood the plight of ordinary folk in the Highlands and Islands. Lord Selkirk was an exception.

"The progress of the rise of rents and the frequent removal of the ancient possessors of the soil have nearly annihilated in the people all that enthusiastic attachment to their chiefs which was formerly prevalent, and have substituted feelings of disgust. The permanent possession which they previously retained of their paternal farms, they consider only as their just right, from the share their predecessors had borne in the general defence, and they can see no difference between the title of of their chief and their own".

Selkirk calculated that *"the spirit of discontent and irritation"* among the Islanders could be channelled into a successful project.

Lord Selkirk's initial plan had been to take pioneers to Upper Canada but the government had unexpectedly withdrawn their support. Land owners had woken up to the fact that this *"epidemical fury of emigration"*, spoken of by Dr. Samuel Johnson, was taking away their labour-force for the lucrative kelp industry. In the opening years of the 19th century the price of this product had reached £20 per ton. As only £1 of this was required for transport charges and £2 to pay the labourers, the land proprietors were making £17 per ton of profit. Dr. Jim Hunter comments; *"A single window in Armadale Castle cost more than a kelp labourer earned in a year"*.

No wonder they did not want to lose their workers! Indeed they did all in their power to oblige them to become dependent on kelp-work. The "Edinburgh Advertiser", a mouthpiece for the landed gentry, trumpeted: *"The rapid strides which emigration is daily making, demands the speediest interposition of government to stop and impede its progress."*

Several leading Skye business-men, tacksmen and ministers had petitioned the King's Majesty in Council for a grant of 40,000 acres of land in America. The Privy Council Committee on Plantation Affairs dismissed the petition on the grounds that it was not desirable for so many people to leave the country.

The Passenger Act, due to come into force in 1803, in the name of providing less crowded and more comfortable conditions, would have the 'side-effect' of raising fares for emigrants. Selkirk promised that his agreed fares would stand and that Prince Edward Island, where he had purchased large tracts of land, was an even better place for diligent pioneers, than Upper Canada or the Carolinas. He was later to boast to government that the people he had chosen for this scheme would otherwise have been lost to the rebellious United States.

Three ships were chosen for the venture: *'Polly'*, *'Dykes'* and *'Oughton'*. Selkirk himself and 200 passengers, mainly from Skye, sailed on *'Dykes'*. MacAulay took charge of 400 Skye passengers on *'Polly'* and a further 200 from Lord MacDonald's South Uist estates left on *'Oughton'*.

To help finance the project, the ships were to return to Scotland with cargoes of timber or wheat.

The outward voyages of the 3 ships were accomplished without incident and, much to Selkirk's chagrin, although the fine new *'Dykes'* was first to leave, *'Polly'*, an older ship, arrived some days ahead of it at Orwell Bay on August 7th 1803.

Lucille Campey says in *"A Very Fine Class of Immigrants"*:

"Selkirk was a lone figure who correctly read the mood of the people. Most Highlanders had to choose between an uncertain future if they stayed put or moved; which effectively meant taking up a job in the manufacturing Lowlands or emigrating. He knew that, faced with that choice, many who could afford their shipping fares would opt for emigration. Much to the dismay of Scotland's ruling classes, whole communities in the Highlands and Islands took the decision to emigrate en masse. The prospect of a better life as transplanted, culturally intact communities proved to be an awesomely compelling goal."

It was thought foolish by some that Selkirk should deliberately choose people from the 'treeless' and relatively mild and damp Western Highlands to pioneer a forested land which suffered harsh and snowy winters as well as very hot summers but, as he had predicted, they quickly demonstrated their natural aptitude for the pioneer life.

He says:

"These had a great advantage over people who are accustomed to better accommodation, and who would have employed a great proportion of their time in building comfortable houses. The Highlanders, on the contrary, had soon secured themselves a shelter, poor indeed in appearance, and of narrow dimensions, but

such as they could put up with for a temporary resource; and immediately applied themselves with vigour to the essential object of clearing their lands. They proceeded in this with assiduity; and though the work was of a nature so totally new to them, they had made a considerable progress in cutting down the trees before the winter set in. The same work was continued during winter, whenever the weather was not too severe and upon the opening of spring, the land was finally prepared for the seed."

Selkirk was certain that success would only come if the settlers were totally self-reliant. Land could be purchased from him but was not leased or given free of charge. The same principle was applied to their provisions. An agent was appointed to purchase food and other supplies for the group until their farms were well established, but the settlers had to pay for this support. Those who could not pay were given assistance in the form of short-term loans.

He believed in the importance of strong community ties and took care to ensure that the various townships were within a reasonable distance from each other, as their homeland communities had been. Each settlement contained self-supporting family groupings and had sufficient spaces left to allow for later expansion.

He wrote:

"It would be also desirable that the lots could be laid out somewhat wide of each other, so that lands of different parties should have some intervals between them, which they could invite their friends to come after them and occupy. In taking several hundred acres, an individual does not imagine he shall cultivate or need it all himself, but he must have room to spread and room for his brother or cousin that is to follow him."

As the Skye and Uist folk were of different religious persuasion, Selkirk took pains to settle them in different parts of his territory. The staunch Presbyterian Skye settlers bought land in

Queens County while the Roman Catholic contingent settled in Kings County.

> *"When people are determined to emigrate, and several in a neigh-bourhood are so inclined, they would find much comfort in keep-ing together, and again forming a little society in their newly-adopted homes. Fifty-seven families might settle in a square of three miles, and each have 100 acres, with 60 over, which the proprietor might give for a school and place of worship. Such a Settlement could maintain a Minister of the Gospel, and Schoolmaster, and employ a good tradesman in each calling, and a pleasant thing it would be to have fifty-seven neighbour-settlers within a mile and a half of the centre of the settlement!"*

J. L. LEWELLIN. CHARLOTTETOWN; 'A Brief Account of a Fine Colony' 1834.

Having arrived at Orwell Cove, the Skye-folk began to build their settlements on lots 57, 58, 60 and 62, extending from the mouth of Charlottetown harbour to the Pinette River. These became known as the Belfast townships. The name was said to be a corruption of the French *'La Belle Face'* and was founded on the abandoned site of the former French colony. The Belfast district was later extended inland, (Lots 50 and 64) and south-ward to include territory from the Vernon River to Wood Islands.

Passengers on 'The Polly'

Old gravestone of a 'Polly' passenger from Skye

I have been unable to discover any list of the Selkirk settlers of 1803, but a list of signatories to a letter in appreciation of Rev. Dr. MacAulay's services to the new community, written in 1811, has been obtained by Mary C. Brehaut from a descendant of Lord Selkirk. These signatories were heads of families living in the new settlement. As mentioned above, from this list we can distinguish all but one of the names of Lord MacDonald's tenants who in 1802, had informed his Edinburgh lawyer that they *"intended to leave for America"*. For our purpose we can identify several passengers who had come from the Braes of Trotternish in the Isle of Skye. It is more than likely that these first settlers, in their correspondence back home, encouraged their neighbours and relatives with news of their new life.

1811 List

Murdoch Gillis*	Malcom Buchanan	Donald MacRae Sn.
Evander MacRae*	Peter Murchison	Hector MacDonald
John MacDonald Sn.*	Donald Gilles	**Donald Murchison^**
Donald Nicholson**	Donald MacKinnon	John MacDonald Jr.
Donald Murchison*	John Murchison	Murdo MacLeod
Donald MacRae	Harry MacLeod	Samuel Martin
Murdoch MacLean	Donald Nicholson	John MacKenzie
Donald MacLeod	John Ross	Donald Beaton
Alexander MacLeod	Donald Ross	Angus Beaton
John Gilles	Samuel Beaton	John Gilles
Donald MacPherson	**Charles Stewart^**	Donald MacInnes
John Nicholson	Allen Shaw	John MacLeod
John Campbell	John MacRae	Roderick MacRae
John Beaton	Kenneth MacKenzie	Alexander MacKenzie
Angus Ross	Donald MacRae	Donald Stewart
Angus MacMillan^	Charles Stewart	John MacPherson
Angus MacDonald	Lachlan MacLean	Malcolm Bell
Donald MacPhee	James Cowrie	Donald MacNeil
Donald MacRae	James Currie	James Munn
Hector Morrison	James MacMillan	Angus Mun
Alexander Martin	Archibald Blue	Malcolm MacNeill
John Bell	John Mun	Angus Bell
Malcolm MacMillan	Finley MacRae	Duncan MacRae

Malcolm Mun	Angus Beaton Sn.	Kenneth MacKenzie Sn.
Hector MacMillan	Finlay MacRae	Alexander MacArthur
Allan MacMillan	John MacDonald	Alexander MacLeod
Dugald Bell	Malcolm MacLeod	Donald Martin
John MacPherson	Murdoch MacDonald	Finlay Odarty
Peter Campbell	Angus Odarchy	Donald Odochardy
John MacRae	John MacLeod	John Buchanan
Alexander MacKenzie	John MacQueen	Alexander Lamond
John MacDonald	Sairle Nicholson	**Donald MacQueen** °
Donald MacLeod	Donald MacLeod	**Martin Martin** °
Hector MacQuary	**Malcolm Buchanan**[2]	**Donald Buchanan** °

*indicates elders. ** indicates the first Schoolmaster. °identified as from Braes from John Campbell's list. ^identified as from Braes from Murchison Forum on-line. (There are undoubtedly several others from the Braes area but this is difficult to prove).

[2]identifies the poet (see next).

Note that the surnames Mac, Mc and upper and lower case 'D','d' etc have been regularised. These English names were alien, even to their owners!

In the poem *'Emigration of the Islanders'* by Malcolm Bàn Buchanan from Flodigary, a passenger on *'Polly'*, we have a first-hand account of, the reasons for his emigration, the sadness of leaving, the excitement of sailing and positive experiences of the new homeland.

Imrich nan Ei l e a n a i c h
Calum Ban MacMhannain

Emigration of the Islanders
Malcolm Buchanan

"An am togail dhuinn fhin
Mach o Chala Phortrigh,
'S iomadh aon a bh' air fir 's iad bronach;
Iad ag amharc gu dluth
Null's an suil air an luing,
'S ise 'gabhail a null gu Ronaidh.
Thuirt Mac Faid as an Dig,
'S e ag eigheach rium fhin,
'"S ann a laigheas i sios gu Trodaidh,
'S biodh am fear a's fhearr tur
Nis 'n a shuidh' air an stiuir,
Gus an teid i os cionn as t-Soain.
Eilean eil' ann da reir
Agus Sgeir na Ruinn Geir,
'S bidh muir air a' bheisd an cdmhnuidh;
Tha cnap eil' ann no dha,
'S ann dhiubh sin Clach nan Ramh,
'S Bogha Ruadh, tha fo aird 'Ic Thorlain;
Leachd-na-Buinne seo shuas,
'S Rugha 'n Aiseig ri 'cluais,
Mol-a-Mhaide 's e cruaidh le doimeig.
Thoir an aire gu dluth
Cumail ard os an cionn;
Seachain sruth Rugha Hunais, 's mor e."

"When we set out
from Portree harbour
there were many sorrowful people on shore;
they gazed across intently
with their eye on the vessel
as she headed for Rona.

Said MacFadyn from Digg
as he shouted to me,
"She will veer down towards Troddady;
let the most capable one
be at the helm
until she reaches beyond Soain.
There is another island too
and Sgeir na Ruinn Geir,
which is usually concealed by the sea.

There is another obstacle or two;
among these Clach nan Ramh
and Bodha Ruadh under Aird 'ic Thorlain,

Leachd na Buinne yonder,
and Rubha na h-Aiseig adjacent to it,
Mol-a-Mhaide with its hard-set boulder.

Dh'eirich soirbheas o'n tuath
Dhuinn os cionn Fladaidh-
chuain,
'S ann a ghabhadh i 'n uair sin
oran;
I a' siubhal gu luath,
'S i a' gearradh ma cluais,
'Dol a ghabhail a' chuain 's i
eolach.
Thug mi suil as mo dheidh
Null air Rugha-Chuirn-leith,
'Us chan fhaca mi fhin ach ceo
air.
Sin 'n uair labhair MacPhail,
'S e ag amharc gu h-ard,
" S mor mo bheachd gur h-e
barr a' Stoir e.'
Moire, 's minig a bha
Mise treis air a sgath
Ann an Rig, 's gu'm b'e 'n t-aite
bho e!
'N uair a thigeadh am Mart,
Bhiodh an crodh anns a' Cham,
'S bhiodh na luibhean co-fhas ri
neoinean.
Bhiodh an luachair ghorm ur,
Nios a' fas anns a' bhurn,
Fo na bruthaichean cubhra,
boidheach;
Bhiodh na caoraich da reir
Ann ri mire 's ri leum,
'S iad a' breith anns a' Cheit
uain oga.

Be very careful
to keep well above these;
avoid Rubha Hunish with its
perilous current."

A north wind arose when
we were above Fladda-chuain;
then she hummed along,
moving rapidly
as she tacked around
to take the main she knew so
well.
I glanced after me
towards Rubh' a' Chairn Leith
and saw only mist over it.
Then MacPhail spoke
as he gazed upwards,
"I do believe it is the top of
Storr."

By Mary, how often
did I spend time in its shade in
Rigg; it was an ideal place for
cattle.

When March came
there would be cattle in Cam,
and grasses grew with the flowers.
Fresh new rushes
grew deep in the burn
under the fragrant, pretty banks.
The sheep likewise

Thainig maighstir as ur
Nis a srigh air a' ghrunnd,
Sin an naigheachd tha tursach,
bronach.
Tha na daoine as a' falbh,
'S ann tha 'm maoin an deigh
searg';
Chan 'eil mart aca dh'fhalbhas
mdinteach.
Chuireadh cuid dhuibh 's a'
mhal,
'S fhuair cuid eile dhiubh 'm bas,
'S tearc na dh'fhuirich a lathair
bed dhiubh.
Ciod a bhuinnig dhomh fhin
Bhi a' fuireach 's an fir,
0 nach coisinn mi ni air brogan.

'S ann a theid mi thar sail,
'S ann a leanas mi each,
Fiach a faigheamaid aite comh-
nuidh.
Gheibh sinn fearann as ur,
' S e n cheannach a grunnd,
'S cha bhi sgillinn ri chunntas
oirnn dheth.
'S math dhuinn fasgadh nan
craobh,
Seach na bruthaichean fraoich,
Bhiodh a muigh ann an aodann
Ghrobain.
Air na leacan lorn, fuar,
'N uair a thigeadh am fuachd,

were there, sporting and leaping,
giving birth to young lambs in
early May.

A new master has come
now into the land,
a sad, woeful matter.

The people are leaving;
their possessions have dimin-
ished.
There remains not a cow to put
to pasture.
Some have been put towards
rent,
others died;
rare were those who survived.

What would it profit me
to remain in this land,
where I can earn nothing by
shoemaking?
I'll go to sea;
I'll follow others
in search of a place to dwell.
We'll get new land
which can be bought,
and we'll not be charged a shilling for it afterwards.
Better for us the shelter of the
forest
than the heather-covered hills
facing towards Grobain.

Sin an t-astar bu bhuaine moin-
teach.

Moire, 's fhada dhuinn fhin

Rinn sinn fuireach 's an fir,

Ged a thogamaid ni gu leoir ann;

'S iomadh dosgainn 'us call

Thigeadh orra na'n am

Chuireadh seachad feadh
bheann ri ceo iad.

Ged a rachmaid gu feill

'S ged a reiceamaid treud

'S ged a gheibheamaid feich gu
leoir air,

Thig am Baillidh mu'n cuairt

Leis na sumanaidh chruaidh,

'S bheir e h-uile dad uainn dheth
comhla.

B'e sin fitheach gun agh

Tha air tighinn an drasd',

'S e 'n a Bhaillidh an aite 'n
Leodaich;

Umaidh ardanach, cruaidh,

'S e gun iochd ris an tuath,

E gun taise, gun truas, gun
trocair.

'S beag an t-ioghnadh e fhein

Bhi gun chairdeas fo'n ghrein,

Oir cha'n aithne dhomh fhein co
's eol dha,

Ach an Caimbeulach ruadh

O thaobh Assaint o thuath;

'S nam bu fada fear buan dheth
sheorsa.

On the bare, unfriendly rocks,
when the cold weather came
the moorland seemed endless.

By Mary, for a very long time
we remained in that land;
although we could raise sufficient
provisions there,
many a calamity and loss
plagued these at times,
so that they vanished into the
mists on the mountain.
Although we might go to market
and sell our herd,
for which we got a fair price,
the bailie would come around
with his cruel summons
and extort the entire sum from us.
A miserable vulture
has now come to us
as bailie instead of MacLeod;
a haughty, harsh brute
without clemency for the
tenantry,
without compassion, pity or
mercy.
Small wonder that he, himself,
has no friends under the sun;
I know no one who is acquainted
with him except Red Campbell
from North Assynt,
and may his kind be short-lived.

Ach ma theid thu gu brath
A null thairis air sail,
Thoir mo shoraidh gu cairdean eolach.
Thoir dhoibh cuireadh gun dail
lad a theicheadh o'n mhal,
'S iad a thighinn cho trath 's bu choir dhaibh.

'Us na'm faigheadh iad am
'S doigh air tighinn a nail,
'N sin cha bhiodh iad an taing MhicDhomhnuill;
'S ann a gheibheadh iad ait'
Anns an cuireadh iad barr,
'S ro-mhath chinneadh buntata 's eorn' ann.

'S e seo Eilean an aigh
Anns a bheil sinn an drasd'
'S ro-mhath chinneas dhuinn blath air por ann.
Bidh an coirc' ann a' fas
Agus cruithneachd fo bhlath,
Agus tuirneap 'us cal 'us ponair.
Agus siucar nan craobh
Ann ri fhaighinn gu saor,
'S bidh e againn 'n a chaoban mora;
'S ruma daite, dearg, ur,
Anns gach bothan 'us buth,
Cheart cho pailt ris a' bhurn 'g a òl ann".

But if you go
across the sea
bring my greetings to my friends.
Urge them without delay
to flee the rents
and come out as soon as opportune for them.

If they could find a time
and means to come over
they would not be beholden to MacDonald.

They would get land
in which to sow crops,
and potatoes and barley would grow very well there.
This is the isle of contentment
where we are now.
Our seed is fruitful here;
oats grow
and wheat, in full bloom,
turnip, cabbage, and peas.

Sugar from trees
may be had free;
we have it in large chunks.
There is fresh red rum
in every dwelling and shop,
abundant as the stream, being imbibed there".

Donald MacQueen°, who had held the tack of Upper Ollach in the Braes district of Skye, and who was one of the 'Polly passengers' mentioned above, was the great grandfather of the author Malcolm A. MacQueen, whose book, *"Skye Pioneers and 'The Island'"* gives us such a wealth of information about the early life of the new colony. Donald and his wife Christina MacLeod, formerly of *Glasphein*, Skye, set up home at *Glasvin*, *Pinette*, PEI, but Donald died at an early age, leaving the young widow with six children. Her resilience serves to illustrate the enterprise of these pioneers. She purchased a one hundred acre farm on the north bank of the river at Orwell and worked it herself until her sons were old enough to divide the property. One of her sons, the eldest, Malcolm, by his diligence, was soon able to purchase a farm for himself. In winter when the marsh was frozen over with thick ice, he dragged his framehouse across to his new property!

Settling Belfast and Orwell

As soon as the settlers had purchased their land they set about its cultivation. Potatoes, oats and vegetables were planted in any open areas and the enormous task of felling the forests to make fields for cultivation began. Hay for stock-feed was made on the extensive coastal marshlands, and the stacks often hauled over the friction-free ice and snow when winter came. Shelter was imperative and that was provided by building 'rude cabins' for the first winter. Logs from the first felled trees were squared, dovetailed and used to form the cabin walls. Any spaces between them were filled with clay and moss and the seams sealed with birch bark. These huts provided minimal shelter from the fierce snowstorms and perishing cold. As time allowed, and using iron nails, made within the settlement by a local blacksmith, they nailed pine shingles on the roof to stop melting snow from making everything inside wet and unusable. Window sizes were kept to a minimum as glass was expensive. The severity of the first winter must have come as a tremendous shock to the settlers as they had little food. The thick ice and bitter cold made fishing impossible and survival techniques and emergency preparations had not yet been mastered, but by the second winter they had secured a bumper harvest and were better equipped.

Lord Selkirk said: *"I left the Island in September 1803, and after an extensive tour on the continent, returned in the end of the same month the following year. It was with the utmost satisfaction I then found that my plans had been followed up with attention and judgment.*

> *"I found the settlers engaged in securing the harvest which their industry had produced. They had a proportion of grain, of various kinds, but potatoes were the principal crop. These were of excellent quality, and would have been alone sufficient for the entire support of the settlement.*
>
> *"I will not assert that the people I took here have totally escaped all difficulties and discouragements, but the arrangements for their accommodation have had so much success that few people perhaps in their situation have suffered less, or have seen their difficulties so soon at an end."*

Naturally, Selkirk was very biased in his opinion, and had not himself had to suffer the privations of that first winter, but the people, encouraged by the lush growth of summer, had their optimism rekindled and continued, through community effort, to make a success of the venture.

EXTERIOR VIEW OF A PIONEER'S HOUSE

After their first winter experience, they quickly learned to secure their homes against the unaccustomed climate. The roofs were improved, ceilings installed and a ply of boards was nailed on either side of the log walls to stop the fearsome draughts. The whole interior in some houses was whitewashed with slaked lime. As well as pleasing to the eye, this annual or biennial coat was very hygienic. The practice became common until wallpaper was introduced late in the century.

Their only means of heating and cooking was at first a log fire with open chimney which tended to draw warm air out of the house, replacing it with fresh but cold air. Later, much more efficient iron stoves were installed.

The simple but healthy diet consisted of oatmeal porridge for breakfast and a main meal of salt cod or pickled herring with copious helpings of potatoes. Gradually buckwheat or barley was introduced to vary the use of the famous black oats, but wheat flour was little used for the first ten years or so. The early settlers first used horn spoons for the porridge or ate potatoes and herring without cutlery, much as had been the practice in Skye. But with time, forks and knives became common. A large teapot was always to be found by the fire or on the stove, as the tea drinking habit, acquired in Scotland, followed them west.

Occasionally the usual repast was supplemented by some game, shot in the forest. Poultry, sheep, cattle and horses were purchased when the settlers had acquired means to barter or pay. These animals presented their own challenges, as fences now required to be constructed. The usual fence was a five bar structure of fir or spruce wood. The rails or longers were twelve foot lengths staked at intervals.

Their bedsteads were also of roughly sawn timber with mattresses stuffed with chaff or hay. Blankets or linen sacks containing, first wildbird feathers and later domestic duck or goose down, kept adults and children relatively warm at night. By the 1820s domestic geese were raised in large numbers for their eggs, down and flesh.

Clothing was far from elaborate, being made of homespun cloth or drugget. Shoes were manufactured in the settlement and were of cowhide, well waterproofed with sheep-fat. J. L. Lewellin in *"Emigration to PEI"* (1826) tells us:

> *"Keeping the family clothed and fed took up a great deal of the family's time. Most of the food would be grown and processed at home. They would cure pork, smoke fish, churn butter, preserve berries and make yeast from hops. Other duties included shearing sheep, knitting and sewing clothes not to mention the washing of clothes. They made laundry soap out of tallow and lye and scrubbed the clothes on washboards. The men went to sea to fish or to the fields to farm and more often than not they would do both".*

At first the only book in the house would have been the Gaelic Bible from which Family Worship was conducted, by each household, both morning and evening. As in the Highlands at that time, the Bible and the Shorter Catechism were the main textbooks from which the children learned to read.

Very soon after their arrival, John Gillis from Skye built a log structure near the old French Cemetery which had the dual purpose of the first church and school. Rev Dr MacAulay frequently conducted religious services there, as well as in private homes.

Both men and women set to in an effort to clear their land of trees. Others who had been fishermen in Skye, put out to sea in boats which were built by skilled local carpenters. In the first few years they discovered that herring, cod, mackerel and other species were very abundant in the sea close to their homes and they soon began to trade with passing American vessels.

The value of the timber on their lots was soon realised, although lack of skill in felling and preparing the logs for transport to the sea led to many accidents and indeed deaths. With axe and saw they soon, however, became expert woodsmen. In 1807 alone, Prince Edward Island exported 1,000 ship-loads of timber to Britain and by 1819, it was exporting 17,000 loads. Lumber became the bedrock of the island economy and encouraged the growth of shipbuilding.

As the clearing of wood-stumps was a longterm project, for several years the food crops were planted between their roots. The *coille dhubh* (black forest) or *coille loisgte* (burnt forest) as they called it, was tremendously fertile. There was no need to dig or plough. The seeds were simply scattered on the fresh soil and the crops grew in magnificent splendour. (The commentator Joseph Robertson, a Loyalist refugee from the Carolinas, tells us that it took eight to ten years for the tree stumps to rot sufficiently for them to be pulled from the soil. *"..and in all that time scarcely any ploughing can be performed."*) The precious potato sets were cut to eke out the available stock and sometimes individual potato 'eyes' were extracted with a goose quill to be grown on, ready for planting. The good soil, mixed with ash from the burning of the redundant tree branches combined to give a yield up to twenty-fold. Famous 'MacIntyre' potatoes were lifted, bagged, transported to the ports, and were soon available for export to the States or back to Britain. As the climate was not as damp as the Scottish Islands, potato blight was not a problem and the scourge of Colorado Beetle did not arise until 1895. An infestation of this pest was to prove as much of a problem to the next generation in Prince Edward Island as blight was to be in both Britain and Ireland in the 1840s.

Gearan an Tuathanaich – The Farmer's Complaint
Was written and translated by Rev. A. MacLean Sinclair

This song is sung to the melody of "Thug mi *n oidhch' an raoir' san àiridh" and was written on December 22, 1896. The song is a straight-forward complaint from a farmer whose back hurts from picking and killing the destructive potato bug.

Tha mi sgìth a togail dhaolag,	I'm tired picking potato bugs
Tha mi sgìth a togail dhaolag,	I'm tired picking potato bugs
Tha mi claoidhte mu na chaol-druim,	I have a pain in the middle of my back
'Togail dhaolag de'n bhuntàta	From picking potato bugs
'S iomadh olc a tha 'san t-saoghal,	There's many an evil in the world
'S iomadh plàigh 'tha tigh'nn air daoine,	And many a plague coming on me
'S iomadh ni' tha milleadh saoithreach.	And many things spoiling farm work
'S a toirt aobhair air bhith cràiteach	And giving occasion to be vexed

Back in the 1820s, as fertility began to decline, due to lack of both rotation and fertiliser, fine silt from the natural oyster-beds in the numerous coves and bays was dug out by large iron shovels pulled by horses, and transported to the fields, which had recently begun to appear in the clearings.

Now that there were recognisable fields, harvesting of the flax, wheat, barley and oats with the sickle or reaping hook between the tree stumps became obsolete. The improved scythe was called a reaping-cradle, but it required great strength as well as skill to operate it, and so it was soon replaced by the first mechanical reaper, drawn by two or three horses. As they had done in their home island, the women and children shared the men's efforts in the fields. Although the work was hard, they soon began to see an ample return for their labour. This was in marked contrast to the lack of reward they had experienced for their equally hard graft in Skye.

The varieties of fruit and vegetables that were now grown on the Island must have been a wonderful experience for people who had only known potatoes and kale on Skye!

An interesting snippet, gleaned from the shipping archives, tells us that on 17th June 1828, the ship '*Margaret & Polly*', commanded by Captain Kelly, sailing for Antigua from Charlottetown Harbour. As well as a cargo of grain and potatoes, there were eight kegs of cranberries! Soft fruit had become important for trade. An area near Belfast which had been swept by fire, burning up the whole forest, was first named the Barrens, only to be later renamed Alberry Plains when wild berry bushes began to thrive in the fertile soil.

It must be remembered that the new settlement was not composed entirely of the Gaelic speaking islanders, but others with very welcome skills were gradually being absorbed into the community. Several Lowland Scots made a very valuable contribution to the new settlements. A certain Alexander Anderson brought the first cart wheels from Lowland Scotland.

'In 1829 there were only three gigs in the occupied townships and each could be recognised by its sound a long way off.'

He was also a pioneer in the introduction of the famous black oats which grew so well in the Belfast district. Other

Lowlanders brought their very important knowledge of flax cultivation as well as their weaving skills. The first Skye settlers had of course brought their own spinning wheels which they had, until then, used principally for making wool products. In those times, a woman who could not spin or knit was something of a rarity!

Waulking or shrinking the tweed was practised in Prince Edward Island as it was in Skye, to the accompaniment of the same Gaelic songs! The thickened cloth or drugget made warm and comfortable, everyday clothing. Several commentators refer to the *'Thickening Frolicks'* as special social occasions when the community gathered to celebrate their Highland heritage. As on Skye, the work song was an encouragement during communal labour but neighbours often met to tell the old tales and to sing Gaelic songs.

MacQueen comments; *"During the long winter evenings young and old gathered in neighboring homes to ceilidh, drawn by the genial atmosphere that pervades certain homes in the community. There they told stories and sang folk-songs. These were in Gaelic, and among them;*

Fhir a' Bhata	The Boatmen
Caber Feidh	Clan Song of MacKenzie
An Gleann 's an robh mi' og	The Glen where I was young
Oidhche mhath leibh	Good night – parting song
Posadh puithir I'n Bhain	Highland wedding song
Horo mo nighean donn Bhoid-heach	My nut-brown maiden
Bu chaomh leum bhi mirreadh	My young brunette
Mo run geal dileas	My faithful fair one"

Alexander Anderson's other important introduction was the first iron plough, which gradually replaced the old wooden ploughs. His son, also Alexander, was later to build up-to-date water-mills on the Newtown River. Although the first mill at Belfast had been commissioned by Lord Selkirk on the Pinette River, it was a Skyeman, Donald Nicholson, son of *"Polly"* passenger John Nicholson, who first erected and operated a grist mill at Orwell Bridge. His new home was at Portree Creek and he was sufficiently prosperous to employ a skilled stone-mason, William Harris from Devon, England, to construct it. Harris later married his daughter. Donald's son Peter, took over as miller from dad. He was always referred to as *"Patrick Sten-scholl"*, this being the part of Trotternish, Skye, that Donald had come from. It is interesting to note that the *Stenscholl Mill* in Skye had been run by the same Nicholson family without much encouragement from the chief of Clan MacDonald, or his new factor!

Sawmills were quickly erected, due to the necessity of providing sawn boards for shipbuilding, houses, churches, schools and the other public buildings which were soon under construction.

When British travel writer Isabella Lucy Bird visited the colony in the mid 1850s, she noted the Island's *'brilliant green'* colours, the *'gently undulating'* landscape, and its *'soft soil'*, all of which made the Island *'very suitable for agricultural purposes,'* although she noted, *'I never heard of anyone becoming rich through agricultural pursuits.'* PEI was, Bird wrote, *'extremely pretty'* — *'small villages, green clearings, fine harbours, with the trees growing down to the water's edge, and shady streams.'* She described Charlottetown as *'prettily situated on a capacious harbour'* and noted that *'everywhere, even twenty miles inland, and up among the woods, ships may be seen in course of construction. These vessels are sold in Britain and the neighbouring colonies; but year by year, as its trade increases, the island requires a greater number for its own use.'*

Earlier Lewellin had stated; *"At present there are a great number of vessels, from 60 to 100 tons and upwards, built in the Colony every season, and sold in Newfoundland for the seal-fishery".*

Schools and Churches

Malcolm MacQueen comments: *"No quality characterised the Scottish race more than their love of education. They realise, as few other peoples, that knowledge is the sesame that opens wide the magic door to a life of wider prospect with all the increased privileges and added sorrows that go with it. Every family strives to give higher education to at least one son. The parents and other children patiently undergo all the privations necessary to attain this desired end. The religious outlook of Scotland, of which their school system is an expression, has done more, perhaps, than any other agency to incul- cate that proud spirit in the race which encourages the young to feel that there is no position in society to which the individual may not aspire."*

As might be expected therefore, the early settlers soon began to provide places for education and worship. As well as John Gillis's church/school at Belfast, Donald Nicholson, the Skye Elder, who came on the *'Polly'*, conducted the affairs of the first school in the Pinette district. Prior to this, well qualified Skye schoolmasters taught in private homes. It was not until 1821 that the Government began to open national schools and 1826 before teachers were required to have certificates of proficiency.

In 1823 Rev John MacLennan, from Ross-shire, not only ministered to his flock at Belfast, but taught all the usual subjects, plus Latin, at the Pinette School. His work was highly commended by the School Inspector in 1841. By then many of the youth of Belfast had gone on to shine in institutions of Higher Education, the professions and in business. MacQueen comments: *"The spirit of their forefathers had taken root in the soil of the new world."*

What Pierre Berton said of the Scots throughout the new Canada, can also be said of those pioneer settlers of Prince Edward Island: *"For the Scots it was work, save and study; study, save and work. The Irish outnumbered them, as did the English, but the Scots ran the country ....They controlled the fur trade, the great banking and financial houses, the major educational institutions and, to a considerable degree, the government."*

With land granted by Lord Selkirk for the purpose, St John's Presbyterian Church, Belfast, was ready for use in 1823 when Rev John MacLennan arrived from Scotland. This much revered pastor and teacher preached over a wide area, travelling often in very difficult weather conditions, but had his home church at Belfast until his well-earned retirement back to Scotland in 1849.

Medicine

As well as his spiritual and political duties towards the early settlers, Rev Dr MacAulay was the only qualified medical man. After his death in 1827 the people had a long period of time without a doctor until Dr Donald Munro came to Orwell from Skye in 1840. As in the Highlands, several of the settlers were skilled herbalists, particularly those of the Beaton or Bethune family. These skilful men and women were able to give some relief for certain conditions, but several epidemics and diseases took a heavy toll on the new and fragile community. Diphtheria, tuberculosis, croup and scarlet fever were as common here as they were in 19th century Scotland.

Dr. MacAulay was one of the first to be buried at Mount Buchanan Cemetery. It then became known locally as *Cleachd an' Leighaich* (The Healer's Burying Ground).

It is fitting that his tombstone was erected by a grateful community.

In Memory of
Angus MacAulay, M.D.
Chaplain of H. Majesty's First West
India Regiment.

He settled Belfast with emigrants
From Scotland in the memorable ship
"Polly" in 1803. He died Dec. 6,
1827, aged 67 years.

Also his wife, Mary, died April 9,
1857, aged 99, daughter of Samuel
McDonald, of Sartle, Scotland, Capt.
In H. Majesty's Army during the
American Revolution.

It is interesting to note that Mary MacAulay's father Captain Samuel MacDonald, tacksman of Sartle, and a near relative of the clan chief, was remembered as a man of significant physical strength. To this day, in the township of Sartle, in Skye, there is a very large stone called *Uallach Caiptin Shomairle* (Captain Samuel's Burden). In the 1970s, a local man, noted for his strength, was just able to lift this stone off the ground. It is said that Captain Samuel could carry it!

Belfast's success was noted in evidence to the 1826 Emigration Select Committee. Its population had quadrupled.

> *"Selkirk brought his colony from the Highlands and Isles of Scotland and by the convenience of the tenures under which he gave the land and by preserving industry on their part ...... the inhabitants are all in easy circumstances and their numbers have increased from 800 to nearly 3000."*

Lucille Campey says of Lord Selkirk: *"Selkirk backed these settlers from Skye because he knew they could take the privations of pioneer life and they, in the end succeeded. The first generation had a diet of heartache and grinding work but for the generations who followed, the rewards were plentiful. It was a remarkable team effort."*

In A. B. Warburton's 'A History of Prince Edward Island' we read:

> *"They [The Selkirk Settlers] were a very fine class of immigrants.... They were an enterprising and energetic people who transmitted their vigorous dispositions and their stalwart physique to their*

children and their children's children. Descendants of these settlers have been distinguished in almost every walk of life....Their sons have distinguished themselves in every profession, trade and pursuit.....Lord Selkirk did well for this Island when he brought these immigrants to its shores."

Memorial to Belfast's 1803 Settlers
(text in Scottish Gaelic)

English translation

Farewell to the land of the hills and the heather,

The land of our ancestors, land of our love,

It is today firmly enslaved

With distress and cries of woe in every place.

The King of Glory will be our hope

And we will find land, freedom and sustenance

In the great wide forests

And every sorrow will disappear.

"The earth and all that is therein belongs unto the Lord."

CHAPTER 7

The Ships That Followed.

"By the 1820s Highland proprietors, who had formerly fought hard to retain their tenants, increasingly swung in favour of emigration schemes although they largely resisted calls to finance their tenants' travel costs until the 1840s."
Lucille Campey

In the years that followed, there were many shiploads of Scots, English and Irish emigrants to Prince Edward Island.

> *"The population of Prince Edward Island ... has progressively increased at a very rapid progress. The population being in 1806, 9,026: in 1827 - 23,766 and in 1833 - 32,292; an increase in 27 years of 22,616 ... since 1833 the population is supposed to amount to about 40,000 persons."*
> J. L. Lewellin in *"Emigration to PEI"*

Many of these new immigrants were Scottish Highlanders, but, although many more came, we hear little of Skye folk joining the early pioneers until 1829. A tale is told however, of Donald Nicholson the Orwell Miller. He was appointed Lord Selkirk's Shipping Agent and arranged the lumber cargoes for shipment back to Britain. He is said to have returned to Skye in 1805 to *"collect his bride"*, Isabella. The outward voyage to Scotland was horrific, as the ship was caught in a violent storm. Returning to PEI in 1806 aboard *'Rambler'* with several of his Skye neighbours, he composed a Gaelic Ballad which related his experiences since leaving the Belfast community. For many years this lengthy poem was well known and would be recited verbatim at ceilidhs wherever Scots gathered.

The versatile Donald later became an esteemed magistrate on the island.

The next ship from Skye, whose passengers were to have a significant impact on the history of Prince Edward Island, was the *'Mary Kennedy'* which arrived on the 31st May 1829.

"Argosy never sailed with more precious cargo than that discharged at Charlestown on June 1st, 1829 from the good ship Mary Kennedy. There were 84 heads of families in the party. These left their native place about six weeks ago in a ship for Cape Breton along with a number of settlers for that Island. They seem all to be in high health, and judging from appearance, in easy circumstances. With prudent foresight characteristic of their race they came provided with 12 months provisions and an ample stock of warm clothing. They all have relatives already settled on the Island, chiefly about Belfast, and, we understand their intention to locate in that thriving settlement." Prince Edward Island Register and Gazette 2 June 1829, quoted in Skye Pioneers. M. A. MacQueen.

"They settled along Murray Harbour Road, and in the Back Settlement, later called Lyndale. Each family bought from 50 to 100 acres of land. They named the Uigg district after their birthplace, Uig, in Skye, famed for romantic beauty, and deriving its name from the Norwegians who held the Western Isles of Scotland for generations." Skye Pioneers. M. A. MacQueen.

"At the time of their arrival, the upper reaches of the Orwell River had no distinctive name, and it was on Ewen Lamont's proposal that it was given the name 'Lyndale' which it bears today. Ewen was himself born in 1817 in Bernisdale in the Lyndale district of the Isle of Skye." The Lamonts of Lyndale. H.S. MacLeod

Malcolm MacQueen states that these settlers, and one of their leaders in particular, Rev Samuel MacLeod, were distinguished for their adherence to the 'religion of the homeland'. *"Their heritage of piety persisted undiminished for several generations in their new home."*

Several of the 84 households, had seceded from the Church of Scotland, following the early Skye religious revivals, to form a Baptist Church and the banner of these Godly pioneers was: *"My Presence shall go with thee"*.

Like so many of their Presbyterian neighbours who had benefited from the preaching of evangelists like the Blind Fiddler, Donald Munro, in the Isle of Skye, these people had very strong faith in Christ and a trust that God would keep them and their families in all their trying circumstances.

Cuir-sa do dhòchas ann an Dia,	Set thou thy trust upon the Lord,
is deanar maitheas leat,	and be thou doing good:
Mar sin sior-mhealaidh tu an tìr,	And so thou in the land ahalt dwell,
's beathaichear thug u beachd.	and verily have food.

Gabh tlachd an Dia, is bheir e dhuit	Delight thyself in God: he'll give
làn rùn do chridh' a chaoidh,	thine heart's desire to thee.
Do shlighe tabhair suas do Dhia;	Thy way to God commit, him trust,
earb ris, is bheir gu crìch.	it bring to pass shall he.

Salm xxxvii V 3-5	Psalm 37 V 3-5

Samuel MacLeod was born in Uig, Skye in 1796 and became the schoolmaster of the local school. At the age of 23, when it became known that he had been baptised by total immersion, the School Board demanded his resignation. He acceded to the inevitable, but informed his masters: *"I am more independent than His Majesty, our King. If he is dethroned he must leave his throne behind, but I take mine with me!"* So saying, he boarded the *'Mary Kennedy'*, carrying his schoolmaster's chair on his shoulder. It is interesting to note that when the author James Hunter visited Prince Edward Island, on his *'Travels among a Worldwide Clan'* in 2004, he met up with a certain Harold MacLeod, a great-grandson of Samuel. Harold was able to show him his great-grandfather's chair which has pride of place in his Uigg home.

Another commentator tells us that the Skyemen who emigrated at this time were careful to bring fishing nets and tools which they believed would be important in their new life in PEI. Communication with their relatives, who had preceeded them, ensured that they were as well prepared as they could possibly be.

In 1830 an article in the *'Inverness Courier'* supports these comments:

> EMIGRATION.—Three emigrant ships have lately sailed from the West Highlands with no less than 1500 passengers, for Cape Breton and Prince Edward's Island. The emigrants are chiefly from Lord Macdonald's estate, and part are from that of Mr M'Leod of Rasay. To the most needy of the adventurers, Lord Macdonald gave £1 each, young and old. Most of the poor islanders have taken their nets with them, in order to prosecute the fishing in the distant country, whither they have gone for an asylum.

In the years 1829 to 1831, a number of other ships embarked for Prince Edward Island with passengers from Skye. *'Louisa'* of Aberdeen sailed via Stornoway with a large number of passengers. 170 of them disembarked at PEI, most settling at Uigg, while the remainder went on to Cape Breton.

'Vestal' sailed via Tobermory with 301 passengers, most of whom were Skye folk. Again many settled in the area of Lot 50

as they had already been able to acquire title to vacant land. The *Inverness Journal* commented at the time that the trip had been organised by *"two respectable agents ... Islesmen themselves – partly as a trading speculation and partly as an act of philanthropy ... not uncommon among better orders in the Highlands."*

In 1831 '*Mary Kennedy*' sailed again, via Tobermory, with 80 Skye passengers.

There were also several other ships, in those years, which collected passengers from the West Highlands and Islands (including Skye).

On 5th June 1830 a letter was opened by the Honourable Charles Grant Highland M.P. at his office in the House of Commons, London with a list of 48 emigrant families hoping to leave soon for Cape Breton and applying for a grant for some necessary implements. The bulk of those listed in the letter, headed by their spokesman Alexander Beaton, did in fact sail to Cape Breton aboard the '*Malay*' and settled at Margaree. Four of the listed families, had actually already sailed to P.E.I. in 1829, probably on the '*Vestal*', and one family, due to particular circumstances, delayed its passage until 1831. However ten of the listed households were believed to have made their way to Cape Breton on another ship but, for some reason, they were persuaded to settle in Prince Edward Island. From the point of view of our detective work, we are particularly interested in these ten families, as we have reason to believe that they were the sailing companions of **Murdo MacLeod from Camustianavaig.**

In Harold S. MacLeod's book *"The MacLeods of Prince Edward Island"* we discover that our Murdoch MacLeod and his two brothers Angus and Alexander arrived in PEI in 1830. From **Letter 1** we know that Murdoch sailed via Tobermory in Mull, which was the last port visited in Britain, before the Atlantic crossing. These facts narrow our search considerably, so that we can say with a fair degree of certainty that Murdoch and his brothers sailed on the ship '*Mary*' (of Newcastle). This ship was commanded by Captain Jacobson and took 36 days in passage, arriving on August 18th 1830. The *'Mary'* carried 330 passengers picked up from Loch Snizort in Trotternish. 64 of the passengers continued on to Quebec, while a few disembarked in Cape Breton.

The names of the heads of the ten families were:

Donald Cameron, **Miles McInnes, John Ross, Donald MacKinnon**, Alexander Finlayson, Duncan Nicolson, **James Nicholson**, Alexander Ross, Duncan MacDonald and Donald McLeod.

[James Nicholson is known to have come from the Island of Raasay and was a relative and close friend of the famous Rev. Roderick MacLeod of Snizort *(Maighstir Ruaraidh)*. Some years later, the Rev. MacLeod himself, came to PEI on a preaching tour and to visit his sister Jessie, who had emigrated from Skye with her husband Donald Murchison. It is not known if Donald and Jessie lived at Lot 67, but Rev. MacLeod stayed at James Nicholson's home there. We are told of an incident which amused James' young children. *Maighstir Ruaraidh* came down to breakfast in bare feet. Of such little incidents is history made!!]

[Author's family connection: -

Donald Murchison (son of Samuel, son of Paul, son of John) was born about 1789 in Bernisdale Skye and died in PEI. He married Jessie MacLeod daughter of Rev Malcolm MacLeod and Mary MacLeod. She was born about 1790 in Raasay and died in PEI. i.e. Jessie was sister of Rev Roderick MacLeod!

Samuel Murchison's sister was Marion Murchison my great-great-great-grandmother!!]

The names of those four emigrants, highlighted above, along with **Murdoch** and his brother **Alexander**, resurface in a district of central PEI then known as Scotch Settlement. This locality, off Anderson's Road, which led from Charlottetown to

Princetown, consisted of most of **Lot 67**, the southern part of Lot 22, and pieces of Lots 23, 24, 30 and 31. (It was earlier named Strathalbyn by some Perthshire pioneers who had swiftly moved on, due to the inhospitable nature and loneliness of the forest.)

The area was later divided into the townships of Breadalbane, Emerald, Rose Valley, Springfield, Springton, Stanchel, Fredericton, Glen Valley, Pleasant Valley and Hartsville. (It's worth noting that Stanchel got its name from Stenscholl in Trotternish, Skye.)

CHAPTER 8

Braes on the Isle of Skye

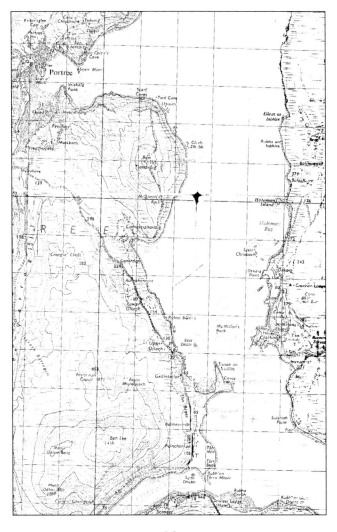

"The crowding of people strongly attached to the land upon even smaller portions of it became intensified and led to the most painful readjustments. The displaced people tended to crowd into neighbouring townships, were moved to the seashore, rented patches of barren land and tried to earn a living by fishing."
I. F. Grant 'Highland Folk Ways'

The 'Wing' of Skye called Trotternish (Tronda's wing) consists of *"The Braes of Trotternish"* immediately south of Portree and *"Iochdar Trotternish"* to the north of the capital. The most southerly point of Trotternish is the headland of *Mol*. There are three parishes within Trotternish, Portree, Snizort and Kilmuir/ Stenscholl.

The first mention of the Braes district that I can find is in a charter of the Earl of Ross in 1349 in which he, styling himself 'Lord of Skye' granted *"terras de Brehe"* to an Adam de Urquhart. The Gaelic name for the area is *Am Braighe*.

The present-day townships of the Braes district were marked out as individual crofts and assigned grazing rights following the survey of the Clan Donald Estates by John Blackadder in 1811.

Peinchorran, Balmeanach and *Gedintailor* benefited from the common grazings on *Ben Lee* and *Meall Odhar*. It was when these traditional grazings were re-let by the MacDonald Estate to a single tenant in 1865 that the placid acceptance of their lot by the crofters began to be replaced by the rumblings of discontent which were to lead to the *'Battle of the Braes'*, sometimes referred to as the Last Battle on British Soil!

Ollach (Upper and Nether), Achnahanaid and *Conordan* shared hill grazings from *Beinn nan Capull* to *Creag a' Chait*; and *Camustianavaig, Peinifiler, An Torran Uaine* and *Inveralivaig* were assigned grazing shares on the slopes of *Ben Tianavaig*.

Both *Upper Ollach* and *Conordan* were not divided into individual crofts but continued to operate as farm tacks after 1811, leased for five years at a time. *Peinifiler* continued as a tack held by Captain Alexander MacLeod until it was split into crofts in 1831. Captain MacLeod, a veteran of the Napoleonic Wars, built Mossbank House in 1782 and occupied it, and its environs, until his death in 1844. He was succeeded at Mossbank by Sheriff Fraser, who continued a small farming operation there.

From the 16th Century, as in most parts of the Highlands, the clan chief, MacDonald in this case, provided for his near kinsmen by leasing them large portions of his estate, called 'tacks'. There were a number of tacks in the Braes area, sublet by each tacksman to groups of joint subtenants.

In the 16th Century, the rental for a penny-land or *fearann peighinn* in these townships was "*6 stones of meal, 6 stones of cheese, 1 cow and eke in money 4s 2d*". Twenty penny-lands were equal to the *tirunga* or *ounceland* (rented for an ounce of silver). Even the penny-land was often subdivided to *lephin* or half penny and *feorling* or farthing land. *Merkland* was quarter land or equal to five penny-lands.

Information obtained from the Clan Donald Centre tells me the following, about my own great-great-great-grandfather in 1733;

> "*John Nicolson of Olich (Ollach) being sworn and interrogated in the Irish tongue (Gaelic), depones that he possesses the half of one pennyland of Olich and pays yearly for the same to Sir Alexander (MacDonald) or his factor forty merks of silver duty, two pound eight shillings scots of cess and two pecks of horse corn and no other casualties whatever and this is the truth as he shall answer to God*".
>
> *Cannot write.*

Until the first half of the 19th Century there were other occupied townships in the Braes district, which were later abandoned as changes came about to the way of life. Many of their inhabitants moved into the newly designated crofting townships. Blackadder's analysis of the Clan Donald Estate had advised that tacksmen were unnecessary and that individual tenants, renting (deliberately small) areas of land, directly from the chief would be more of an asset to the Estate. Their rents would help swell the coffers. Up to that time, these *lesser tenants* (sub-tenants) knew little about money, as most people on the Island had operated a barter economy, and any agricultural produce was mainly for home consumption. How could they pay rent unless they could earn wages? Fishing for herring was one earner, but the arrival of the herring shoals or schools could not always be relied upon and the local boats were required to sail farther and farther from home. Rev Coll MacDonald, the parish minister, commented in the 1830s;

> *"The herring fishing, some years ago, was carried on here with considerable success. In a fine evening in the month of July or August when all the boats belonging to this parish* (Portree) *and the adjacent parishes of Glenelg, Lochalsh, Lochcarron, Applecross, Gairloch, and Loch Broom ... from fifty to seventy sail in number, appeared in the Sound of Raasay, a most delightful scene was exhibited. But the most agreeable and most useful of all exhibitions was their return to the harbour the next day, deeply laden with the richest and most delicious herrings."*

But by 1841 the minister reported that the decline of the herring fishing had contributed to the destitution of the people of his parish in 1836-37.

The answer to everyone's problems, as far as Lord MacDonald was concerned, was the kelp industry! He needed kelpers and the people needed money to pay his rents. The kelpers were obliged to move to the coastal townships where the *'golden fringe'* grew. Indeed more families moved to these townships than there were crofts for them! As a result, subdivision and overcrowding became common and a growing number of landless cottars began to build houses in these communities. Their presence was tolerated by the Estate, while it was in its interest!

The pattern of modern crofting townships, instituted in 1811, is *"profoundly unlike what preceeded it"*.

It is said that Sir Walter Scott related a conversation he had had with a tacksman; *"I have lived in woefull times; when I was young the only question asked concerning a man of rank was – how many men lived on his tack – then it was, how many black cattle it could keep, but now it is how many sheep will it carry"*.

The older settlements used the traditional system of common cultivation and shared working, which had fitted in well with the social organisation of the clans. These joint-farms varied in size according to the land available for cultivation and grazing. The precious *'in-field'* was under constant cultivation on a run-rig system and required to be separated from the more sterile hill-side by a head-dyke. These turf-dykes, *'gearraidh fail'* were originally constructed at six feet in height and were essential for keeping the animals from the growing crops in spring and summer. (A Justice of thePeace Court held at Sconser in 1788 ruled *"all marches of earthen dykes shall have two faces 6ft high. Dykes of drystone are to be 4¹/₂ft and kept in repair the whole year".*)

The joint-tenant farm has been described as *'like a common-wealth of villagers'*…. *'Each of them was inhabited by persons nearly related, who were always on hand to come to each others' assistance and in some instances carried on all of their work in common.'* (Douglas; Observations on the Present State of the Highlands)

The Gaelic word *'baile'* can mean a cluster of houses, a village, a hamlet, a clachan or a farm, while the *'buaile'* was the livestock fold or paddock. These *'buailtean'* remain as a significant feature, even in today's landscape, as they still differ in vegetation colour due to the *'tathing'* or manuring they received from the wintering stock, or from rotational manuring with seaware. To see examples of these parks or folds we need only use 'Google Earth' which gives us significantly better views of the old clachans than can nowadays be seen on the ground! The *'baile'* and the *'buaile'* were features of the joint-tenant farm. The parks probably all had local names at one time. There are a few in Braes which are still remembered; *buaile a' chreagain, buaile a' cnàmhag, buaile a'gròbare, buaile na sliseagan* (park of the wood shavings), and *am buaile ruadh*.

In 1776 Pennant remarked that *"the greater tenants (tacksmen) keep their cattle (black cattle breeding stock) in winter in what are called winter parks, the driest and best grazing they have; here they are kept till April, except the winter proves very hard, when they are foddered with straw: in April the farmer turns them to the moorgrass which springs first, and at night drives them into the dry grounds again"*.

From the 1st of May, *'Beltain'* the black cattle were driven into the hills to graze peacefully until the young-stock was sold in autumn, as only a minimum number of cattle could be over-wintered. It is interesting to note that the autumn Portree Cattle Fair was established as early as 1580!

J MacDonald writing his *'General View of the Agriculture of the Hebrides'* in 1811, says; *"The Isle of Skye has hitherto been wholly devoted to pasturage"*.

Although farming in Skye was indeed mainly pastoral, some crops were grown and indeed, very little meat was eaten, the people preferring a diet of oatmeal, dairy products and fish. Martin Martin writing in 1703 had commented; *"There is no place so well stored with such quantity of good beef and mutton where so little of both is consumed by eating"*.

The introduction of potatoes around 1750 was a welcome life-saver for the poor, but the people came to overly rely on this crop, so that in the years when the potatoes failed, starvation was the inevitable result. 1835 and 1836 were known as the Destitution Years, due to poor harvests, when most crops suffered. By 1841, a total of 32,000 barrels of potatoes were grown in the Portree parish alone, so that we can appreciate that the Potato Famine of 1845 had a devastating effect on the population here, as it did elsewhere in the British Isles.

In the old townships around *Ben Tianavaig* we can still clearly see in the 'in-fields', the signs of former cultivation by the method known as *feannagan,* lazybeds or rigs. The thin soil was ridged up to help with cropping and drainage. Cultivation was achieved using the *Cas Chrom* or foot plough.

To increase fertility, seaweed was hauled from the shore in creels, chiefly by the women. The method of allocation of the strips of land was known as run-rig. Each family took part in a ballot which ensured that the system was fair. If you had a poor strip of land in year one, you might be more fortunate in year two. However, such a system did not lend itself to land improvement, as there was little incentive for a family to increase the long-term fertility of a patch which would next year go to a neighbour.

It was a characteristic of those times however, that the poor and aged were not forgotten by the community. Portions of land called *cionagan nam bochd* were set aside for those not capable of tilling the soil. These areas were cultivated by friends and neighbours, who also cut sufficient peat fuel for their winter use.

It is interesting that Skye's local, now international, Gaelic Rock Band, Runrig, has taken its name from this system of land use.

Housing

"Thoir dhòmhsa sìth, is gràdh, is gaol,

Ri taobh nan sruthan tlàth,

Mo bhothan beag fo sgàil nan craobh,

'S mo lios ri taobh na tràigh."

"Give me peace, charity and love,

Beside the gentle streams,

My little cottage under the trees,

And my garden beside the sea."

Neil MacLeod (Niall Dhòmhnaill nan Òran)

A Skye 'Blackhouse'

Many of Skye's literary visitors of the 18th and 19th centuries have had much to say, but little complimentary, about the conditions in which the ordinary people lived. The houses were very often dismissed as dark and dirty and referred to in a derogatory fashion as 'miserable huts'. The poets Coleridge, Southey, William and Dorothy Wordsworth all visited Highland bothans. Dorothy took quiet pleasure in *"observing the beauty of the beams and rafters gleaming between the clouds of smoke, crusted over and varnished by many winters till, when the firelight fell upon them, they were as glossy as black rocks on a sunny day cased in ice"*.

In the days of the joint-farms, most houses in Skye had the dual purpose of housing the family and their domestic animals. One door allowed access; animals to the left, humans to the right. To the 21st century reader this sounds most primitive and unhygienic, but there were decided advantages, not least the warmth from the cattle providing 'central heating'! The milk cow, a couple of goats and one or two of the *'caoraich bheag'* (little sheep as opposed to the *'caoraich mhor'* the big commercial sheep brought into the Highlands from the Scottish

Borders), were the usual occupants of one end of the house. Dr. Colin Sinclair in his book *"The Thatched Houses of the Old Highlands"* tells us that the 'black house', *"calls for no elaborate description as it was of simple form and humble dimension. It furnished but the bare essentials for people whose material needs were few. Bounded by four rude walls, its fireplace was set in the middle of the room, its lighting was scanty and hygienic devices were absent. Furnishings were governed by utility rather than luxury; a box-bed, a dresser with presses and plate-racks, a bench or settle, a meal barrel and a water-stoup. The three-legged pot was suspended over the fire by the 'slabhraidh' – a chain attached to a crossbeam of the roof"*.

The bed mattress was usually made of sacking filled with heather or straw but later these were substituted by chaff.

Around the peat fire, the ceilidh was held, songs were sung and ancient tales re-told, while the women spun the wool and knitted garments.

The sign of a good housewife was summed up in Gaelic as: *'Cas air creathaill 's làmh air cuigeil, comharraidh na deagh mhnà-tighe'*. Foot to cradle, hand to distaff.

Katherine Stewart, in her book *'Crofts and Crofting'* makes some interesting connections between the people and their housing conditions: *"In spite of the crowded conditions, or perhaps because of them, there was a delicacy of behaviour between the sexes and between generations, a dignity of bearing which was marvelled at by travellers of the time and which perhaps stemmed from the aristocratic structure of the old clan society.*

> *"Strangers were welcome as they had always been. A very old Gaelic poem has these lines: 'I have put food in the eating place. I have put wine in the drinking place ... For often comes the Christ in the stranger's guise ....'"*

Alexander Smith in *'A Summer in Skye'* (c1857) observed *"two bare-footed and bare-headed girls yoked to a harrow and dragging it up and down a small plot of delved ground."* This incident prompted him to compare the lives of the native Skye peasants with city dwellers of his day. His descriptions and conclusions paint a lively picture of the social conditions of the poor in the mid 19th century. First of all he talks of the discomfort of the 'Skye hut', as he calls the native, thatched 'blackhouse' of the time. *"During my wanderings I had the opportunity of visiting several of these dwellings and seeing how matters were transacted within. Frankly speaking, the Highland hut is not a model edifice. It is open to wind and always pervious to rain. An old bottomless herring firkin stuck in the roof usually serves for a chimney, but the blue peat-reek disdains that aperture and steams wilfully through the door and the crannies in the walls and roof. The interior is seldom well lighted – what light there is proceeding rather from the orange glow of the peat-fire, on which a large pot is simmering, than from the narrow pane with its great bottlegreen bull's-eye. The rafters which support the roof are black and glossy with soot, as can be seen by the sudden flashes of firelight. The sleeping accommodation is limited and the beds are composed of heather or fearns. The floor is the beaten earth, the furniture scanty; there is hardly ever a chair – stools and stones, worn smooth by the usage of several generations, have to do instead.*

> *"One portion of the hut is not unfrequently a byre and the breath of the cow is mixed with the odour of peat-reek and the baa of the calf mingles with the wranglings and swift ejaculations of the infant Highlanders. In such a hut as this there are sometimes three generations."*

Having described the inadequacies of the 'black house' he turns his attention to the positive side.

> *"Am I inclined to lift my hands in horror at witnessing such a dwelling? Certainly not! I have only given one side of the picture. The home I speak of nestles beneath a rock, on the top of which dances the ash-tree and the birch. The emerald mosses on*

its roof are softer and richer than the velvets of kings. Twenty yards down that path is a well that needs no ice in the dog-days. At a little distance, from rocky shelf to rocky shelf, trips a mountain burn, with abundance of trout in the brown pools. At the distance of a mile is the sea, which is not allowed to ebb and flow in vain; for in the smoke of the house there is a row of fishes drying; and on the floor a curly-headed urchin of three years or thereby is pummelling the terrier with the scarlet claw of a lobster. Methought, too when I entered I saw beside the door a heap of oyster shells.

Depend upon it, there are worse odours than peat-smoke, worse neighbours than a cow or a brood of poultry; and although a couple of girls dragging a harrow be hardly in accordance with our modern notions, yet we need not forget that there are worse employments for girls than even that."

A common Gaelic expression for the homeliness of the *'bothan beag'* was *'cul ri gaoithe, aghaidh ri gréine'* (back to the wind, face to the sun).

It is clear that there is no happy medium when the blackhouse is described by the literati!

In this same period, Sheriff Nicolson was writing of the inhabitants of these homes, his relatives and friends.

"Reared in those dwellings have brave ones been;
brave ones are still there.
Forth from their darkness on Sunday I've seen
coming pure linen,
and, like the linen, the souls were clean
of them that wore it.
See that thou kindly use them, O man;
to whom God giveth
stewardship over them in thy short span,
not for thy pleasure!
Woe be to them who choose for a clan
four-feeted people!"

The 'four-footed people' were the sheep which the land proprietors had begun to bring into the Highlands, in order to heap up profit from their wool, at the expense of their clansmen.

Reconstruction of one of the old settlements showing a cluster of houses, 'in-fields' and 'out-fields'.

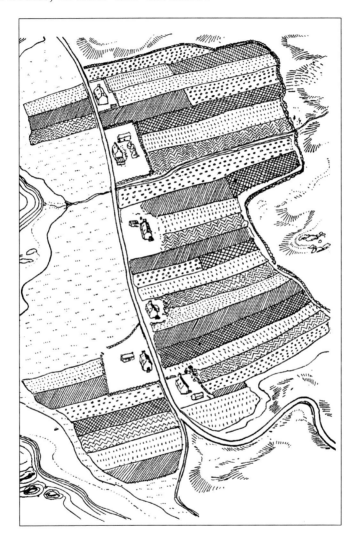

Contrast the post 1811 Crofting settlement with clearly separated holdings along the roadside.

Some of the 'old settlements' in the *Peinifiler* and *Camustianavaig* area were *Scorr, An Achadh (Achadh nan Scuir), An*

Gorstain, Muchclach, Lac Buidhe and *An Gleannan*. On examining The Clan Donald Estate rental records for 1833/34, I found reference to another township named *Totaig* neighbouring *Peinmor* and *Peinifiler*. The name was new to me, but I soon realised that this was a non-Gaelic speaker's attempt at *Tota-Thaoig*, (literally Taog's ruins). These were the ruins of the 16th century home of a man, *Aodh Mor Maccuinn*, famed for his physical strength and mental abilities. Taog (like the Irish Taig) MacQueen was bodyguard and adviser to Donald Gorm, Chief of Clan Donald at Duntulm Castle and was granted a tack of land in Portree parish.

All activity in these old townships had been carried out on a communal basis, but from time to time the local tacksman would call on his tenants to plough, plant or harvest for him. The few animals kept by the sub-tenants provided milk, eggs, meat and wool for the hamlet. Oats and short-stemmed bere barley were planted but it was imperative that the animals were kept from the growing crops, so a system of transhumance was practised. After planting time in spring, the animals, herded by the women and young people would set off for the moorland *airigh* or shieling for their summer grazing. The men-folk remained at home to cut peat for winter fuel, re-thatch the houses or put out to sea for the fishing. The *airigh* huts themselves had to be repaired annually and sufficient peat cut, dried and stacked for the shieling cooking fires of the following year. The milch cows, goats, sheep and poultry enjoyed the sweet grass and heather diet and the cows' milk was made into butter, crowdie and cheese. Casks of fresh butter were stored in the peat bogs to exclude oxygen and preserve the product for use in winter. The shieling system ensured that full use was made of all the hill-grazing available to the township and also preserved the grass closer to home, and at lower altitude, for the leaner seasons of the year.

There were several shielings in the Braes area, still identifiable, each one belonging to its own particular township, some on the slopes of *Ben Tianavaig* and others between *Ben Lee,*

Beinn nan Capull and *Creag a' Chait*. All were within two miles of their home clachan. Some of the names remain in folk memory; *an airigh dhubh, airidh na coille* and *airidh a' ghlinne*.

Malcolm D. MacSween's thesis on *'Transhumance in North Skye'* tells us that the original shieling huts were

> *"remarkably uniform over all of North Skye. For the most part, the bothies are circular or near-circular in shape, entered via a single door, with a smaller opening within, giving access to a similar adjacent structure of lesser dimensions. They were built principally of turf for occupation in the fine season only".* When one was excavated it was concluded that there were; *"one or two courses of rough boulders at ground level, with the remainder constructed of turf. Many of the huts observed surmounted mounds or 'tells' of considerable proportions – in places up to ten feet in height. This indicates continued occupation of the same site over a considerable period......They are largely composed of peat ash and other occupation material".*

The roof structure appears to have been similar to that of the winter dwellings in the townships – *"a few beams of bog-timber covered with sgrathan (thin turves), thatched with raineach (bracken), fraoch (heather) or muran (sea-bent), held by acraichean (anchors) of stones tied to sìomain-fraoich (heather rope)".*

MacSween also mentions pillows of *canach* (bog cotton), a bench of turf, recesses for the storing of household utensils and an open fire. *"The lesser chamber fulfilled the functions of a dairy storehouse".*

Structures of this sort can still be identified in Braes, on knolls which remain remarkably green. Beneath *Beinn nan Capull,* one such structure is beside a waterfall called *Eas na Màthraichean* (the mothers' waterfall, where the laundry was performed).

The trip to the shieling was regarded as the highlight of the year and was attended with great cheerfulness.

It was not uncommon for the young people to *ceilidh* on their neighbours in the other, nearby shielings or to fish for trout on the lochs and streams. MacSween says; *"The rich and varied folklore woven around the airigh, the love songs and fables – all testify to the summer movement being a time of gaiety and relaxation and a welcome change from the drag of life in the clachan. The shielings with their attendant gatherings, made wider intercourse possible, and must have helped to keep the Gaelic tongue alive"*.

It seems likely that this form of transhumance had begun in very early times when the Picts or early Celts had moved their grazings to the hills, from *La Bealtuinn* (1st May) to *La Samhuinn* (1st November). These were fire festivals of the ancient Druid religion. The Celtic god was *Beil*, from which we get the Gaelic words *Bi* and *Beatha* (being and life). The name Beltain Festival comes from *Beil-teinne* (fire of Beil). On May 1st, all the winter fires were extinguished and the spring fire relit to signal the returning of the sun, which was worshiped by the Druids as their most powerful god. All the cattle were required to pass through the smoke of the spring fire and the household fires were kindled from the sacred flame. On November 1st a new fire was lit as a farewell to the departing sun of autumn and again the cattle had to pass through the smoke. Household fires were never allowed to go out, day or night!

"Nuair thig a' Bhealltuinn,	"When Maytime comes,
'S an Samhradh lusanach,	And the leafy summer,
Bidh sinn air àirigh	We will be in the sheiling
Air àird nan uchdanan;	On the height of the braes;
Bidh cruit nan gleanntan,	The lyre of the glens,
Gu cainntir, cuirteasach,	Will be sweetest and dignified,
Gu tric 'gar dùsgach	Often rousing us
Le surd gu moch-eirigh."	With the joy of early morning."

William Ross

The shieling system in the Braes area was probably destroyed by separate letting of the hill grazings to sheep farmers. Crofting tenants were banned from the hill in some parts of the MacDonald Estates.

'*Penifiler and Heatherfield Reflections*', published for the 2000 millenium, by the residents of these modern townships, tells us about the clachans or townships of former days;

"Achadh a Scuir – Only the crumbling ruins and the tales passed down through the generations are testament to a thriving hamlet which once existed in this beautiful spot in the front face of Ben Tianavaig. Even the earliest Ordinance Survey maps ignore the presence of this once busy little community. It would appear that the inhabitants were cleared from this area with their only option being to resettle on the coastline, possibly as cottars, eking a living from fishing or the kelp industry.

"Sheriff Fraser of Mossbank, who died in 1877, took an interest in this small community and they wintered his horses for him until one year a heavy snow fell and the horses died in snowdrifts. The valley beside the hamlet is known today, in Gaelic as 'Gleann na Cnàmhan', the Glen of the Bones.

"With the menfolk often away at the fishing, the day to day work of running the collective farm was left to the women and included carrying half-bolls of meal from Garbh Cammas up the steep winding path to their homes, the best part of a mile.

"A little lower and to the south of An Achadh, lies An Gorstain which suffered a similar fate with the people moving, in the 1830s, mainly to Camustianavaig, though at least one family went to An Torran Uaine.

"Scorr was, by far, the largest of these communities and supported five large crofting/fishing families in 1833 and in the census of 1861 a population of 31 people was still recorded as living there. Life was hard in this north-facing enclave when there would be little sun in the winter months and the dwellings were at the mercy of northerly gales. Open peat fires provided heat for the

heather-thatched cottages and also for cooking the daily meals. As the fires had to be alight all year round, it was essential that fuel provision was made in the spring and summer to cut, dry and stack sufficient peat to ensure a plentiful supply for winter months. In the poor arable ground, turned by means of the 'cas chrom' (crooked spade) the crops grown were potatoes, hay and oats.

"Herring was not just an important part of the crofter's diet, both fresh and salted, but also provided an opportunity for men to earn a living at fishing or net-making in Portree. The nimble-fingered women could also contribute to the household by filleting the herring and packing the salt barrels for transport south and abroad. With their own own supply of milk, butter, crowdie and salt meat, the Scorr people were largely self-sufficient and could also supplement their diet by shooting ducks and cormorants which abounded round the coastline. Seagull eggs were also collected in early May, primarily for use in baking.

"Two heavy blows struck this fragile community. In 1841 the Rev. Coll MacDonald reported that the decline of the herring fishing had contributed to the destitution of the people of his parish in 1836-37. In the 1840s the herring had still not returned and it was then (1846-1853) that the second blow struck when potato blight devastated the staple food on which the people had come to rely.

"Added to their problems was the collapse of the kelp industry and their inability to pay the ever increasing rents.

"Scorr was eventually deserted in 1846 when there were no longer sufficient men to pull the boats ashore".

CHAPTER 9

The History of Lot 67 PEI

Strathalbyn's Jubilee
"Hail to the Pioneers: Strathalbyn's men!
On whom, and their descendents God doth smile
Who left old Scotland's shores to plant again
Free homes and hearts on Lone Prince Edward Isle

They brav'd the dangers of the mighty deep
For months they sailed the Atlantic's misty way
But well they knew their God, His watch would keep
Their Polar Star by night, their guide by day.

Excelsior! Our watchword ever be!
In God we trust! And crave his blessed smile
Thus all our sons be ever brave and free!
God bless Strathalbyn and Prince Edward Isle!"
Respectfully dedicated to Rev. M. Campbell, Strathalbyn, PEI
By John Imrie, Toronto, Ontario.

Much of this information is gleaned from a speech made
by the Honourable A. B. MacKenzie on the occasion of
the Strathalbyn Jubilee in 1895. The whole affair was
quoted in detail in 'The Daily Patriot'.

By 1895 only two men and six women of the 1830 pioneers
were still alive, but MacKenzie also mentions the presence of
widow Mrs Murdock MacLeod, whom he mistakenly assumes
had come in 1830 with her husband. She, of course, is Effy

MacLeod, Murdoch's wife who arrived with their children, in July 1840, probably aboard *'Nith'*. (see later)

I make no apology for quoting freely, large parts of a very long speech, as it gives a distinct flavour of the lives and hardships of these pioneers. I've highlighted references to our Murdoch MacLeod and his family.

"Early in the summer of 1831, a large band of stalwart young Highlanders, chiefly from the Isle of Skye, accompanied by their families, emigrated to Prince Edward Island. (At that time sparsely settled with a population of about thirty-two thousand people, while Charlottetown was but a village, with a population of about twenty-five hundred people). Some of these settled in the Southern part of Queen's County, while some twenty families, induced by the prospect of purchasing land in fee simple, and on easy terms, decided to settle on Lot 67, which at that time, with the exception of the Haslam family on the north end of it, was an uninhabited and unbroken wilderness, covered with a beautiful dense forest of heavy hardwood, spruce and pine. Unmolested, save by the paw of wild animals, the land enjoyed its Sabbaths.

"Taking into account that these people were unaccustomed to the use of the axe and other conditions unavoidable in their new and untried circumstances, and taking into further account that the only approach to their new quarters was by a bridle path, along blazed trees, from Alexander Johnston's on the Princetown Road — a distance of seven miles to Springton where now your beautiful manse stands. The pioneers must have been endowed with more than ordinary courage to face the hardships and trials confronting them; but as the most of them had some means to tide them safely over the first year, as well as pluck and self-reliance, the prospect of buying their farms at reasonable rates more than outweighed their doubts and fears.

"The names of the first pioneers given were Miles McInnis, Donald McKinnon, James Nicholson, Donald and Alexander

Martin, John Ross, Peter Stewart and his son John, Malcolm McDonald—a grand type of the old venerable Highland Chieftain, and his three sons, Donald, John and Alexander, Malcolm McLeod, John McLeod—another type of the Highland hero, and his son Donald, lately deceased, Lodwick McIntosh (MulDonish), a man of patriarchal bearing and appearance and his four sons, Roderick, John, Alexander and Donald, and John Matthewson and his father Jonathan, who was the first man who died and was buried at Springton, **Murdock McLeod (joiner) and his brother Alex, who is still hale and hearty though over eighty years of age, he is the father of education in the settlement,** *and Donald and Angus Beaton. These were joined a year or two afterwards by Angus McDonald, John McDonald, Angus and Ronald Stewart, John Cameron, George Cahill, Nathaniel Kelly, Robert Todd, Neil McKinnon, Donald McLeod, Malcolm McLeod and his brother Alexander, and John McLeod.*

"As all the northern part of Lots 31, 65, 29 and 30 save a small portion at the north end—as well as the eastern ends of Lots 23, 26 and 27 were still and for some years after an unbroken wilderness; their nearest neighbors to the west were the Wrights of Middleton, on the south Victoria, on the east the McNeils of North River and Alexander Johnston and the Haslams and the Bagnalls on the north. (**Note that in Letters 1&3 Murdoch's address is c/o Squire Wright.** Charles Wright was himself a landlord, but also attorney for Louisa Augusta Fanning, Lady Wood, who was the major landowner in lot 67, following her father Edmund Fanning's death in 1818. He had been Lieutenant-Governor of the Island.)

"Their effects had to be carried on their backs from Johnston's during the summer months, until the Anderson Road was opened in the years 1833-34. Their first care was to clear a little patch of ground whereon to erect their first cabins, which consisted of small structures of round logs—twelve by sixteen feet covered with spruce bark; the interstices between the logs being stopped

with moss or clay with a small hole dug in the ground for a cellar and a capacious chimney, the lower part of which was built of rough stones with a wooden mantle piece, and the upper part or smoke stack of cats, which consisted of pats of clay mixed with straw fastened on small round sticks placed horizontally tier after tier until it reached about two feet above the roof. This superstructure in a very short time became so very flammable that great care had to be exercised to prevent a general conflagration. I am not informed as to how these hardy veterans endured the rigor of the first winter in their new quarters, but one thing is certain they did not suffer from cold as they had abundance of the best fuel at their doors.

"Towards the month of April however, the settlement was the scene of much activity. The men and boys busy from sunny morn till dewy eve chopping trees and clearing the land to plant their first vegetables in, while the brave women and young lassies were equally busy making maple sugar. Being an enterprising race of men they set to work in dead earnest clearing the forest; as the land at that time was very productive, the following autumn yielded to them an abundant return for their spring's labors. In a very short time many of them were proud possessors of square log houses, covered with either boards or good split pine shingles. After getting well settled their next care was to build a schoolhouse at Springton on a plot of land given to the settlement for that purpose. Their first schoolhouse was a rather primitive and crude structure, but it was an earnest of better things yet to come. Well do I remember the ruins of this old school house, which in after years was used as a temporary lodging place for some new arrivals who afterwards came to the place, Yes, I believe it was the birthplace of at least one prominent man who may now be within the reach of my voice. It was a round log house, twelve by sixteen, covered with bark or turf. It had one window of six panes 8 x 10. Their first teacher was **Mr. Alexander McLeod (Alaister Beag)**, who is still alive. As the tenure of his office was before I was born I am not informed as to his success as a knight of the birchen rod.

"*During the first few years the people had no slated means of grace among them. Mr. James Nicholson, who was a bosom friend of the Rev. Dr. Roderick McLeod of Snizort, from the beginning of the settlement, and for some years afterward held a prayer meeting alternately in his own house and Lodewick McIntosh's every Sabbath, where he read and expounded the word to those who came to listen?*"

"*The Rev. Robert Patterson, visited the settlement in the summer of 1837 and preached a sermon in the open air near James Nicholson's house on which occasion he baptized several children. I am informed that the Rev. John McLennan of Belfast visited the settlement the same summer but held no public religious services. In the year 1837, the Rev. Donald McDonald visited the settlement and preached then and occasionally for some years afterward in Donald McLeod's house, until his people built a church in the year 1847. Many of his hearers came under the power of his preaching. Their old church was torn down about 30 years ago— but I understand his adherents have a new one in course of construction in Stanchel, a new school district, carved out of Springton and Rose Valley school district. In the year 1837 a larger and more commodious schoolhouse of square logs covered with shingles was built. It was about twenty-four by thirty feet and had two windows of 12 panes, 8 x 10. It was used the following seven years as a meetinghouse as well as a schoolhouse. The first teacher who taught in the new schoolhouse was James Douglas, of Stanhope. As he could not speak the language of Eden (i.e. Gaelic) and but very few of his scholars could speak any other language but the vernacular, his task from the outset was not an easy one, but with the small advantages they had and a keen thirst for knowledge they soon made rapid progress in acquiring a fair command of the English language. Mr. Douglas remained with them for three years. After him they secured the services of Malcolm McDonald, a prim little body, who had just arrived from Scotland and who was equally at home in speaking Gaelic, English and Latin. Being a strict disciplinarian he very often got*" *himself into trouble with some of the larger boys, who very often became impatient at being flogged by so diminutive a specimen of humanity. Rather than submit to the degradation of being denuded of their breeches, his efforts to chastise them, in that primitive war, frequently resulted in the culprit showing flight, and if not strong enough, some of his boon companions who had frequently submitted passively to a similar ordeal, would come to the rescue, when poor Neby would have to beat an inglorious retreat a wiser if not a better man. As he was not the proud possessor of a watch, to gauge the time for dismissing his weary and listless flock, in the autumn days, when the sun was overclouded, he resorted to a very strange devise to obviate the need of a timepiece. He would send one of the boys out for an armful of dry ferns, which he would burn in the chimney and then he would turn to look at the window, and if he could see the reflection of the blaze on the window glass he would dismiss them at once, assured that it was near dusk. But on dark and very cloudy days the experiment often turned to the advantage of the boys who sometimes got home some hours before sundown.*

"In the year 1833-34 the new Bedeque Road, or as it was after-wards called for many years, "The Anderson Road", named after the Hon. Alexander Anderson of Bedeque, who surveyed the line, was opened, from McNeill's, North River towards North Wilt-shire, which was then unbroken forest, thence to Scotch settlement, thence through to what is now called Southwest or Bedeque.

"The opening of the new road was a great boon to the settlers, as it not only gave them means of communication with the outside world, but also afforded them an opportunity of replenishing their exhausted exchequers—by earning money at building the road. About this time some of them had so far advanced in material prosperity as to have a horse or a yoke of oxen, with which to haul their grist to the nearest mills. Previous to this time querns or hand mills taken from the old country were used by some to convert their grain into meal. In a very short time some of them had

become expert shingle makers and others became adepts at sawing boards with the whipsaw. The lucky owner of a horse, a cart or a wood-sleigh, became freighters and charged five shillings, or eighty cents for bringing a load of shingles, boards or any other commodity to Charlottetown. In addition to the eighty cents he was to have three treats of rum or whisky, one on arriving in the Town, and the second on leaving and the third on the way home, but very often these terms were not strictly adhered to, by some of the more generous carriers, as very often they would draw on the five shilling so much that both got gloriously happy over the proceeds of the load that they returned home as empty handed as they left.

"Their farming implements were chiefly made up of the following articles, a good Roger's or Weatherby narrow axe, a hoe, a reaping hook, a grubbing hoe, a flail, a frow and spoke shave. After a few years a yoke of oxen, a straw collar and wooden hames for the horse, a pair of cart wheels, wood sleigh and slide ear, a V shaped harrow with wooden teeth, a hand rake and a big pot for the double purpose of making soap and boiling maple syrup were added.

"In the summer of 1838 another ship band of emigrants from Scotland landed in Charlottetown of whom some thirty or forty, mainly Skye, families cast in their lot with their fellow countrymen in Scotch settlement. These late arrivals settled in what is now called Hartsville, Johnson Road, Lot 22, Rose Valley, Lot 67. Though they had in a measure to contend against similar hardships with the first settlers, yet they had the advantage of the friendship, experience, and assistance of those who came first, as well as the advantage of the new road, opened some six years before. Among these people were a considerable number of God-fearing men, men who were converted under the preaching of such ministers as Dr. Roderick McLeod (Maighstir Ruaraidh) of Snizort, Skye, Dr. Kennedy, of Red Castle, (An Chaistel Ruadh), and Dr. McDonald of Ferintosh (The Apostle of the North).

"Among these I may mention the names of Alexander McLeod, the Preacher, and his brother, John, John Gillis (An Sercam) and John Matheson, the father of the late Angus Matheson. Immediately after his arrival Alexander McLeod took an active lead in conducting religious meetings, not only in the Springton schoolhouse, but also in private houses, in the different localities, in which his countrymen had settled, often preaching in the open air, or in a grove of woods.

"In the summers of 1840-41 there were still a further accession of some fifty families of emigrants from Scotland who joined their old neighbors in the new settlement; these settled in the western part of Rose Valley, Johnston Road (east) Brookfield, West Line Road, East Line Road, Hazel Grove, Junction Road, Colville Road, and Dock Road. Among these newcomers were also men of eminent piety, notably, Murdoch Buchanan, who for three or four years had settled in Bonshaw, after which he removed to Springton, and was one of the first three elders who composed the first session at the formation of Strathalbyn Congregation whose Jubilee we are today celebrating. Although Mr. Buchanan could not read, I believe he could recite from memory the greater part of the Old and New Testament; also **Murdoch McLeod (Murachadh Beag), (Murdoch and Effy's son)** *who settled in New London, but who from his arrival in the country closely identified himself with his countrymen in the Scotch settlement. He was a man of rare intelligence, a good Gaelic and English scholar, equally conversant with both languages, but above all, he was a true and honest Christian, in every sense of the word. He was an orator of no mean order. He was really the first evangelist to Strathalbyn, and was for some years engaged in catechizing and preaching the word in the different settlements I referred to. When he would be on the rounds both old and young, would be in a flurry refreshing their memories on the questions of the shorter catechism. I believe he was instrumental in doing more real good in the place than perhaps any other man.*

"Mr. John McNeill, a Gaelic and English teacher, sent to Cape Breton by "the Society for the Propagation of Christian Knowledge" in Glasgow, Scotland, in the year 1830, who, after remaining in Cape Breton for a few years in a place now called Orangedale, removed to this Island, and settled in Bannockburn, where his religious influence was soon felt for the good, among the scattered children of the Presbyterian families, in that and the adjacent settlements, of West River and Long Creek. During the summer months of the following six or seven years he preached to large audiences, in the Scotch settlement. He was a profound reasoner, and mighty in his exposition of the scriptures and earnest in his exhortations and direct appeals to the heart and conscience of his hearers. Under his able preaching of the word, as well as that of the fore mentioned Murdock and Alexander McLeod, a wave of religious awakening passed over the place and scores of men and women, who afterwards became pillars and shining lights in the congregation, of whom the most have gone home to glory, ascribed their first awakening about their soul's salvation, to the faithful preaching of these lay preachers.

"In 1843, at the time of the Disruption of the Free Church from the Church of Scotland, the people here were generally so well posted on the questions agitating the mother church that they without hesitation decided to throw in their lot with the Free Church party.

"In the summer of 1844 a public meeting was held at which it was unanimously agreed to commence the building of a church forthwith, and within a short time the work was completed. When well seated it would hold from five to six hundred people. For some years after it was first occupied the seats consisted of pieces of scantling, planks, or boards laid on blocks of wood.

"The sacrament of the Lord's Supper was dispensed for the first time in the congregation in July 1845, by the Rev. Alexander Farquharson, of Middle River, Cape Breton. He was one of that

small band of the Church of Scotland ministers in Nova Scotia and P.E. Island who came out with the Free Church party at the disruption. The services commenced with the fasting and prayer on the previous Thursday. Friday was occupied in discussing the questions, Saturday in preparatory services; the Sabbath, the day of ordinance, was a memorable day followed by thanksgiving on Monday. All services were solemn and impressive, the evening services continued till late in the night. On the occasion the solemn rejoicing and religious fervor that pervaded the assembled multitude would aptly remind one of the return of the children of the Captivity from Babylon to build the walls of Jerusalem.

"The first ordained missionary was Rev. Alexander McIntyre. He came from Scotland in 1848, and was stationed for two or three years between Brown's Creek, New London and Scotch settlement. He was a powerful and zealous preacher. He left this Province in 1850 and emigrated from Scotland to Australia where he died ten years ago.

"Contrasting the scanty privileges and opportunities enjoyed by our noble sires and grandfathers with the glorious ones we now enjoy, we may well blush with shame that we do not improve them as we ought. To think for a moment of the hardships encountered by these hardy pioneers in making a comfortable livelihood for their families would today make the heart of the bravest of us quail. So much so that if the Herculean task of clearing the forest were left to the present generation of young men, instead of our beautiful Island home being the gem of the Gulf, the beautiful garden of the Dominion, as it certainly is now, it would forever remain covered with its primeval forest, the abode of wild animals."

We obtain further information on the development of Lot 67 from the 'History of Presbyterianism in Prince Edward Island' and from the 'History of Rose Valley United Church Centenary

1876 – 1976'. These documents, while mainly concerned with the religious development of this part of the Island and the new churches required as the population of the 'Scotch Settlement' grew, tell us much about the development of schools and the value and emphasis that the settlers placed on a good education for their children.

Other important sources of historical interest are the accounts of land purchases in this part of the Island. As mentioned previously, Edmund Fanning, former Lieutenant-Governor of the Island, died in 1818. His considerable land-holding in Lots 50, 65 and 67 was divided among his three daughters, Maria, Margaret and Louisa. Like so many of the aristocratic proprietors, these ladies were somewhat reluctant to dispose of their assets at the prices which the British, and later the Island and Canadian, governments offered. In 1875 these *'Lady Landlords'*, among others, were forced to vacate their remaining holdings when they were compulsorily purchased by the Island government. Prior to this however, individual settlers were able to reach agreement for the purchase of the farms which they had at first rented from these owners.

An indenture dated May 26, 1864 between Roderick MacKenzie and Dame Louisa Augusta Wood states that Roderick Mackenzie leased approximately 100 acres of land in lot 67, named parcel 61, for the yearly rent of 5 pounds, eleven shillings and two pence. The parcel is described as:

> *"by a line commencing at stake placed in the north side of the Anderson's Road at the southwest angle of fifty acres now or lately held by Donald Matheson. It runs thence north one hundred and one and a half chains to the Road,.....aforesaid, and thence following the side of the Road Easterly to the place of commencment, the said courses being according to the Magnetic variation of the year one thousand and seven hundred and sixty four (1764) agreeably to a plan of the said premises in the margin of those attached."*

Rent was to be paid yearly on the first day of January to Dame
Louisa Augusta Wood, her Heirs or Assigns, or to her attorney
at a place appointed by her attorney. The first due date for rent
was January 1, 1865. Roderick was also required to pay the
land tax and all manner of taxes, assessments and impositions
whatsoever, parliamentary or otherwise. This document was
signed by Roderick MacKenzie and witnessed by Charles
Wright, Dame Louisa Augusta's attorney. It was notarized by
Allan Bethune. On the face page of the original indenture there
is written the name of one Duncan MacKenzie dated December
30, 1882, stated as a deed. The 1880 Prince Edward Island
Atlas shows Duncan MacKenzie living on this parcel of land at
that time. Roderick MacKenzie is listed as living on this land
prior to May 26, 1864. Roderick's wife was Catherine MacLeod.
Family verbal history states she lived to be 107 years of age.
The 1901 lot 13 census states that she immigrated from Scotland in 1845. Family verbal history further states that she was
from the Isle of Skye.

Regarding the proprietor of the land leased by Roderick
MacKenzie in Lot 67, Rose Valley/Springton, PEI; Lady Louisa
Augusta Wood was the daughter of General Edmund Fanning,
Lieutenant Governor of PEI from 1786-1805 and Phoebe
Maria Burns. She lived on PEI during her childhood and moved
to England with her family circa 1805. Louisa was married at
Ealing, County of Middlesex, England 28 June 1830, to Sir
Gabriel Wood, a General in the British Army. She died in Bath,
England on 19 March, 1872.

The following is taken from the Abegweit Revue page 53 - Fall
1990, Volume 6, Number 2.

*"Dame Louisa Augusta Wood, as a young girl resided here with
her father and evidently became interested in the MicMac Indians
of PEI. By her last will and testament, bearing the date May 5th,
1870, she gave to trustees appointed by her, 2,573 acres of land on
lot or township 67 in Queen's County, to be sold and the proceeds*

held in trust, one half for the education of the deaf and dumb and the other half for the Indians of PEI."

The second land record of interest is that between Lodewick McIntosh (previously mentioned), who haled from Trotternish, Isle of Skye, and Lady Wood.

(Ludvic is such an intriguing name that I had to do some more research in the Skye rent books. In the long-forgotten township of Eskadale in *Sgoirebreac* in 1823, there were three crofts. No.1 was tenanted by a Ludvic Buchanan, No.2 by Archibald MacIntosh and No.3 shared by Donald Nicolson and the widow of Donald Finlayson. All these tenants left in 1830. Is this a massive co-incidence? Did Archibald MacIntosh's son marry a daughter of Ludvic Buchanan, his neighbour, and did the couple have a son Ludvic, named after his grandfather? The Strathalbyn Jubilee documents tell us of the MacIntoshs and Buchanans who arrived from Skye in the early 1830s.)

This Indenture *made the fifteenth day of October in the year of our Lord one thousand eight hundred and thirty three Between Louisa Augusta Wood consort of Sir Gabriel Wood, late of Prince Edward Island and Maria Matilda Fanning and Margaret William Tryon Fanning of the same Island of the one part and Lodewick McIntosh of the aforesaid Island of the other part....... Witnesseth that for and in consideration of the sum of twenty-five pounds sterling money of Great Britain to the said Maria Matilda Fanning in hand paid by the said Lodewick McIntosh at and before the enseuling and delivery of these presents the receipt whereof the said Maria Matilda Fanning .... assigns all that tract, piece or parcel of land situate lying and being in Grenville parish in Queens County in the same Island bounded as follows that is to say commencing at a square post fixed on the North side of the New Road leading to Bedeque known by the name of Anderson Road marked number eleven thence running North for the distance of one hundred chains thence West for the* *distance of ten chains thence South to the said road and thence following the course of said Road Easterly to the place of commencement containing one hundred acres, a little more or less, and is part of Lot or Township number Sixty-seven (No. 67) once numbered twelve on the plan of said Township.......... unto the said Lodewick McIntosh and his heirs, In witness whereof the said parties to these presents have hereunto set their hand and seals by Samuel Nelson Esquire their true and lawful attorney the day and year first above written.*

Signed, Sealed and delivered
In the presence of Jos Ball.

CHAPTER 10

Gaelic Culture

"Cumaibh suas a' Ghàidhlig,	"Let's keep up the Gaelic,
Cainnt ar màthar fhéin,	Our own mother tongue,
Chaoidh na leigibh bàs i	Never let it die out
Ge b'e cearn d'an téid,	Anywhere you go;
'S i rinn òg ar taladh	It rocked us asleep once
Chuir a gràdh an géill	And ensured our love
Ann am briathran blàth	In its words as warm
Mar ghaoith a' Mhàigh troimh ghéig".	As May's wind through the trees".

This rallying song was composed by James N. MacKinnon of Prince Edward Island.

While Gaelic continued in PEI, to be the language of the home and the church, increasingly English became the language of the workplace. Parents, with ambition for their offspring, encouraged their development through the medium of English, much to the detriment of their mother tongue. This trait parallels what was happening, at a somewhat slower rate, back in the 'Old Country' and Gaelic in Prince Edward Island gradually became the language of nostalgia. This decline was much more rapid than in Cape Breton. However, it is true to say that in the 'backland Skye settlements' such as Lot 67, fluent speakers of Gaelic were still common in the 1930s and 1940s and there were some, in these areas, that could speak only Gaelic into the late 1930s. By the 1950s the last generation, who were more comfortable in Gaelic than in English, was dying out, but some notable, individual fluent speakers and storytellers were recorded for posterity by Dr. John Shaw in 1987. When Rev. John Ferguson of Portree visited the Island in 2003, he was told that the last fluent Gaelic speaker, Percy MacPherson, had recently passed away. Percy's people had come from Skye and both his parents and his grandmother had used Gaelic as the everyday language in the family home while he was growing up.

It has become popular to blame the institutions such as churches and schools for the decline in the language and culture, because of their encouragement of English, but Rev. Donald Nicholson, a native of Hartsville tells one tale of support.

"The first settled minister in Hartsville Congregation – or Strathalbyn as it was called at the time – was linked with Clifton/New London. This man, Alexander Sutherland, when he came out, did not have sufficient Gaelic to preach in that language. In Strathalbyn, practically the entire congregation were Gaelic speakers and most of the older people understood only Gaelic. An elderly man, who had been asked by him to pray, expressed the fear that it was because they had grievously sinned, that God had sent them a minister who could not speak to them in their own tongue. Another parishioner informed the minister who, determined to correct the situation, took time off to return to Scotland to polish up his Gaelic. He returned, competent to preach both in Gaelic and English."

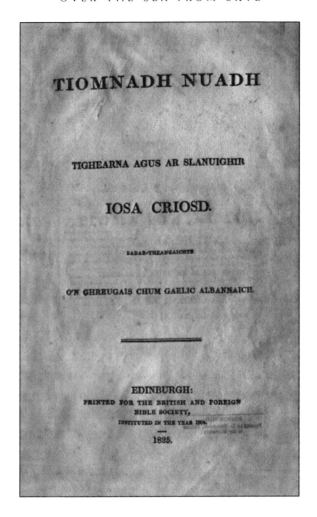

A Gaelic New Testament

The mainstay of literacy was undoubtedly the Gaelic Bible as well as certain religious books which were to be found in most homes. Boston's *'Fourfold State'*, Bunyan's *'Pilgrim's Progress'*, the Gaelic Hymns of Dougald Buchanan and Peter Grant and, of course, the Shorter Catechism, which was learned by heart. Other than *'Sàr-obair nam bard Gaelach'*, the only secular

Gaelic publication which became available before the end of the 19th century was 'MacTalla', a Gaelic newspaper published in Sydney, Nova Scotia. With so few books available in the language, it is therefore astonishing that so many of these people, through several generations, women as well as men, could read and write Gaelic fluently.

The tract societies of Edinburgh and Glasgow saw to it that much spiritual food was supplied to the pioneers; but in English!

The fact that Rev. Samuel MacLeod, although of an Independent Baptist persuasion, offered the version of the Gaelic Psalms approved by the Church of Scotland, ensured that many Highlanders were attracted to his ministry. Lucille Campey says; *"old-country links were preserved, but the religious needs of his New World congregation were also being addressed."*

The Presbyterian Gaels, as well as Samuel MacLeod's Baptists, continued the Scottish practice of unaccompanied singing of the Psalms of David. Since copies of printed Psalmody were scarce, both in the Highlands and in the Colonies, lining-out by the precentor was employed. The preciding minister would read out the first two lines of the first stanza, which were then sung by the precentor-led congregation. Thereafter the precentor would *"intone each verse of the Psalm, one line at a time, in a sort of chant, which might be either traditional or improvised; after the line had been precented, the congregation sang it to a traditional tune, which did not necessarily bear any melodic relation to the precentor's chant. The tempo of the singing was slow and solemn and stresses were marked with heavy crescendos. Trained musical judges describe the effect as maestoso."* Charles Dunn continues by stating that the position of precentor in a congregation was one that attracted particular respect. The Gaelic singing added to the solemnity and dignity of the church services.

Other aspects of the Gaelic culture, with the exception of dance and instrumental music, survived well in Prince Edward Island. Story-telling, '*Beul-aithris nan seanar*' ('the tradition of the elders'), folktales, or unwritten history, was recited, and second generation Islanders would weep at mention of the Cuillins of Skye, although they had never been there, or indeed, ever seen any mountains! Among the tales were Heroic Ballads and lengthy stories of the *Feinne*, (Fingalians), companions of Fingal (*Fionn McCoul*). Many of these tales had been passed on, from one generation to another, at the firesides in the Braes houses and shieling bothans. There were many traditions of the *Feinne* in the area around Portree Bay. Above *Shulishader*, the hill is *Aite Suidhe Fhinn* or Fingal's Seat, where it is said the Irish giant-hero used to sit while directing his deerhounds *Bran* and *Fraoch* in the chase.

A letter sent by Frances Tolmie, a collector of '*The Old Songs of Skye*' to Miss Emily MacLeod of MacLeod at Dunvegan Castle on 18th April 1872, records that '*the heroic ballads are known to the poorest classes*'.

> "*Beinn Ianabheig (Beinn Thianavaig), a peaked hill above the Bay of Portree, was once called Beinn Gulban, where Diarmad, the friend of Fionn, was mortally wounded when measuring the boar. At Sgor is the grave of Diarmad; and at Benmore (Peinmor) is Tobar an Tuirc (Well of the Boar), from which, when dying, he besought Fionn to fetch him a drink. Margaret MacLeod, a poor forlorn cottar woman at Portree, knows these places and can sing the songs about them.*'

Directly connected with this we have a tale recorded by Joe Neil MacNeil of Cape Breton, which was told to him by Archie Kennedy whose father Murdock Kennedy emigrated from Scotland, very likely, Skye. The tale is '*The Death of Diarmid*' and how he was poisoned by touching a sharp bristle while measuring a boar, which he had killed at Fionn's request. These tales often mentioned specific locations in the homeland as a means of adding authenticity and keeping alive the sense of place and belonging which is so characteristic of the Celtic people.

Gaelic songs and poetry also continued to be popular and, in both Prince Edward Island and Cape Breton, *Bàird Baile* (local poets) would compose songs to commemorate special happenings. Gaelic proverbs, expressions and rhymes were remembered and taught to the children. As in Skye, certain homes were popular *ceilidh* houses where neighbours would meet socially. Lucille Campey tells us; *"But, although fiddles and bagpipes provided early settlers with much-needed entertainment, these pioneers kept their memories of homeland alive principally through their churches. Their faith offered spiritual support and continuity with the past."* She goes on to quote Rev James Souter referring to Highland settlers; *"Although they are indeed in a strange land, and lament the necessity which led them to leave a country endeared by so many tender ties and recollections: — but, give them their church, their minister, and their school, and they become, after a time, quite reconciled to the land of their adoption."*

In Roman Catholic districts Highland music, both piping and fiddling, and also dance survived much longer, because Presbyterianism frowned on these 'worldly' activities. Donald Munro, the Skye evangelist, whose disciples many of the pioneers were, had been known as the 'Blind Fiddler'. At his conversion he had burned his fiddle. A similar story is told of Prince Edward Islander, Angus *(Saor)* MacLeod. He was also a noted exponent of the fiddle but was admonished by Rev. Donald MacDonald to *'put aside the violin as belonging to the flesh'*. He took it out and destroyed it with an axe!

Another aspect of Highland culture which seems to have survived in the Maritimes, probably without people realising that it was connected to ancient religious beliefs, was the requirement for fishermen to always turn their boats clockwise or 'sunwise'. The sunworshipping druids believed that the east was the source of all motion. The sun rises in the east and moves toward the south, so man's position is established as 'facing the east'. This makes *'Deas'* the south, as it is at his right hand *'Deas lamh'*. If he then turns toward the south, he is *'deis-eil'*, meaning ready. To move *'tuaitheal'* (northwards) came to be thought of as unlucky. *'chaidh an gnothach tuaitheal'* (the thing went wrong)!

In the early 1900s, at the age of 87, *Peggie Neill* of Orwell Bridge was able to recall that; *"all the original settlers conversed in Gaelic. Although times were hard our wants were few and simple. It may be that not knowing luxuries we never craved them. The only pleasures women had were in the 'ceilidhs', which I suppose correspond to the modern 'teas'. The neighbouring men and women gathered at each other's homes. The Highlanders were all fond of singing and music. At these ceilidhs tales of witches and ghosts were told so vividly that we were often afraid to go home in the dark. Many of the women used snuff and some smoked the pipe. People were hospitable and one could always count on a warm welcome in every home. The church was the great meeting place, where old friends saw each other on Sunday."*

Were all the pioneers happy in their new homeland? Were any sufficiently homesick to attempt to return?

A tale is told of a John MacLennan from the Isle of Raasay. He and two brothers, Ronald and Murdoch arrived in Hartsville, Lot 67, in 1855 and moved in with an uncle for their first year. After the year had passed; *"John began to feel that he had been mistaken in leaving the old country and he got lonesome and wished to return."* He packed his belongings and a cousin agreed to take him by ox cart to a cattle vessel that was scheduled to leave the island. John's planned departure, however, was regarded as a major mistake by his relatives and neighbours and his cousin consequently took the longest possible route to the wharf, passing the time in Gaelic conversation and long stories. They arrived in time to see the ship departing under sail some 500 yards from the shore, and had to return home. This was the only instance known to Rev. Donald Nicholson of a settler from Lot 67 wishing to return to Scotland, and the story has it that John never again mentioned returning to the old country. A few months later *'he and his two brothers took up land in the Scotch Settlement.'*

CHAPTER 11

1840 emigrants

"'S e seo Eilean an aigh
Anns a bheil sinn an drasd'
'S ro-mhath chinneas dhuinn
blath air por ann.

Bidh an coirc' ann a' fas
Agus cruithneachd fo bhlath,
Agus tuirneap *us cal *us
ponair.

Agus siucar nan craobh
Ann ri fhaighinn gu saor,
'S bidh e againn *n a chaoban
mora;

'S ruma daite, dearg, ur,
Anns gach bothan *us buth,
Cheart cho pailt ris a' bhurn *g
a òl ann".

"Tis a beautiful Isle we
inhabit the while,
Naught we plant in its soil
grows sparely;
Oats will flourish with ease,
wheat will wave in the
breeze;
Cabbage, turnips and peas
grow fairly,
And our sugar is free coming
out of the tree,
And we'll have it in chunks
to quarter;
And there's rum to be got in
each bothy and cot,
Just as plentifully as water".

Malcolm Buchanan

From 1839 to 1841 many ships sailed from Skye to Prince Edward Island. The *'Pekin'* of Liverpool, a brig sailing via Stornoway, arrived at Charlottetown on 21st August 1839, with 266 passengers from Skye. A number of these settled in Lot 67. In August of the following year the *'Nith'*, commanded by Captain Shaw, took some 400 passengers on board at Uig and 150 at Tobermory. 97 of them disembarked at Sydney while

315 went on to Charlottetown. Most of these settled at Belfast. They were; *"all in good health, the chief part of them have some property and are likely to become good settlers."*

I believe that **Effy MacLeod and family** sailed on the *'Nith'*.

Within a few days it was the turn of the schooner *'Rother'* and Captain Hall which landed 229 passengers, mostly for Belfast. *"They seem all in robust health and we have no doubt will prove themselves to be a hardy and industrious class of settlers."*

The *'Royal Gazette'* of 24th August went on to say about the Skye folk; *"They are a hardy vigorous set of people – not a pauper among them. Two other vessels from Tobermory are looked for Daily."* One of these was the *'Heroine'* of Aberdeen with 281 passengers. She sailed via Stornoway, arriving in Charlotetown 37 days later. I have failed to trace any information on the other.

In June 1841 the *'Ocean'* of Liverpool with Captain George MacKenzie, sailed from Portree with 335 passengers all for PEI.

In September the *'Inverness Courier'* was telling its readership; *"It gives us pleasure to state that the John Walker and the Washington, two vessels which left Uig in July last with a great number of emigrants, had a prosperous voyage across the Atlantic, and arrived safe at Quebec and Prince Edward Island. These vessels were chartered and fitted out under the superintendence of Mr Archibald MacVicar, the spirited and intelligent emigration agent at Tobermory."*

Meanwhile in Charlottetown, the *'Royal Gazette'* was recording their arrival;

"On July 6th 1841 the 1660-ton sailing ship 'Washington' with a complement of 850 passengers departed from Uig, Skye. The crossing was completed in a record 22 days, arriving at Charlottetown, PEI on July 28th where morning and evening worship were held on the Sabbath Day."

The *'John Walker'* with 10 Skye families (49 persons), did not in fact, call at PEI but took these *'farmers and farm labourers to join their relatives in Glengarry'*.

Emigration from Skye had certainly become "An Unstoppable Force"! When John Bowie, lawyer for several Highland estates was called to give evidence to the 1841 Emigration Select Committee, he gave the following account; *"Since 1837, I have with reference to estates on Skye, been the means of removing a population of 1,850; 600 of those were conveyed to Australia at the Government's expense, the remaining 1,250 have gone to our North American possessions, principally in Prince Edward Island and Cape Breton. The parties preferred these districts in consequence of many of their countrymen having previously settled there; and in consequence of the representations sent home to them, last year there were 700 or 800 went from Skye; and the parties had not been long in their new country before they wrote home such favourable accounts to their friends, that parties are now anxious and many are now actually arranging to go out as soon as they can procure the means."*

Newspaper adverts, encouraging Highlanders to go to Prince Edward Island, continued to appear along with quotes from those who were *'doing well in Canada'*.

A certain John MacCallum wrote in 1851 of his family's increased prosperity; *"My father little dreamed, as he often told me that, when he was carrying on his back 15 or 20 miles a single bushel of potatoes around the margin of the shore, he should live to see the day when he would be able to drive his carriage from one end of the Island to the other."*

And John MacKenzie, visiting from Scotland in 1880, was amazed at the sight outside a Presbyterian church. *"Imagine nearly 200 carriages, four-wheeled, scattered all around the church. It was such a sight as I never saw and never could have seen in the Highlands; yet here there is hardly a family which does not drive to church and market in a nice light wagon or carriage; but in spite of all this, mistaken people at home will advise the poor crofter not to emigrate to a country where such things are possible to those who came out a few years ago in a state of penury and want."*

NOTICE TO EMIGRANTS.

Prince Edward's Island.

PERSONS wishing to Emigrate to British America are particularly recommended to turn their attention to PRINCE EDWARD'S ISLAND, which is situated in or near the entrance of the Gulph of St Lawrence. One of the many advantages it possesses over the Canadas is the clear and salubrious air, and the climate, at all seasons, is healthy, and free from the intermitting fevers and agues so prevalent in Canada. It is surrounded by the sea, which abounds with all kinds of fish. The soil produces crops equal to any in the North American Colonies. The coast around the Island is indented with fine Harbours, and the interior is intersected with Rivers which meander through the richest natural Forests in every district, while springs and streams of the purest water everywhere abound.

The Subscriber having become the proprietor of a large tract of good land, and being anxious to facilitate the Settlement with a Scotch population, now offers land for sale on the following terms:—Farms of from 50 to 500 Acres, at the rate of 20s per Acre; 550 Acres and upwards, at 12s. 6d., if purchased in a block, one-half to be paid down, and the remaining half in six years, with interest. To persons unable to purchase, Land will be given on Lease, at the rate of 1s per Acre, paid annually, with privilege to purchase at any time during the currency of the Lease.

Common rate of wages at Prince Edward's Island is as follows:—For Mechanics, from 80s. to 100s. per month; for Labourers or Farm Servants, 3s. 6d. to 5s. per day, from 50s. to 70s. per month, and £30 to £36 per annum; for Servant Women, 15s. to 20s. per month—the employer in all cases finding Bed, Board, and Lodging.

Exclusive of the other valuable varieties of fish, the Cod fishery is a great source of wealth; any industrious man, having two boys, may fit out at an expense not exceeding £50, and kill and cure 200 Cwt. of Fish, which will sell for 15s. per Cwt. £150, and thereby in six months clear £100 as remuneration of himself and two Boys.

The Subscriber will furnish those intending to emigrate with a passage from Inverness to Liverpool, by steam, about the 15th April, and from thence direct to Prince Edward's Island, at the rate of £3 10s for Adults, and Children in proportion—in a good and approved Ship, accompanied by the Subscriber, who will pay every attention to the comfort of the passengers on the voyage, and will guarantee those emigrants who accompany him immediate employment after landing. Emigrants will no doubt appreciate the advantage of sailing from Liverpool, in comparison to the risk and danger of going north about. The Subscriber will be happy to meet intending Emigrants at Mrs More's Lodgings, and to give every necessary information.

Reference to Alex. Mactavish, Esq., Banker and Solicitor.

ALEX. DAVIDSON.

Inverness, 23d March, 1841.

Thomas Wilson of Charlottetown wrote home in 1818;
*"I am happy you have heard from our sister Catherine and that they
are all doing well here.... The only drawback is the long winter for
the frost comes on about the middle of December and continues till
about the first of May....Please send my black coat and britches as
they will be useful to some of the family....My family all seem to grow
uncommonly fast for I do not think that you would know them
already for the short time they have been out of your sight whether it
is the climate or the change of food I do not know but it is very whole-
some here."*

Among the passengers who arrived from Skye in 1841 were the
grandparents, aunt and mother of a Mrs Marion MacDonald,
who was persuaded to address the Friendly Circle Senior Citi-
zen's Club of Murray Harbor in the 1960s on *"PEI Women
Past and Present"*. She gives a fascinating account of how the
Island developed for the ordinary folk over 120 years.

*"I'll start with what my mother told me about her parents and two
children, coming to PEI from the Isle of Skye, Scotland. After a
rough journey of nine weeks they landed in Charlottetown on a
Saturday night, August 28, 1841. Nephews then living in the
Belfast District met them at the boat. Their parents had come over
on the "Polly" in 1803. They spent the winter with their nephews,
and the following spring bought a densely wooded shore farm at
High Bank. When they cut the first tree at the shore, having difficulty to dispose of it by pushing it down the bank, grandmother
said; 'Thank God for that much clearance'.*

*They built a log cabin, which was heated by a fireplace made
of stone from the shore. They did their baking by putting flat
stones in the fireplace and covering the cooking or baking utensils
with a flat stone. The utensils used were pots and frying pans made
of iron. There were no lamps, and tallow candles made by the
women, lighted the cabin. There were only two wells in High
Bank at the time, both at least a mile from where they lived. They
got their drinking water from a spring at the shore. Women of the*

district took turns, the first summer, washing their clothes at the shore. One woman looked after the children, while the other four women got a fire going at low tide to heat the wash water. As the bank was between sixty and sixty five feet high, this was easier and safer for them than for them to try and carry the water up such a high bank.

There were no roads, only trails where one could go on horseback or walk: no churches, school, or post office. The only cleared land was what they had cut the first spring. They uprooted trees so they could plant potatoes brought from Scotland. They cut the eyes out of the potatoes with a goose quill for planting and saving the rest for food. The women planted the potato eyes and the potato crop proved to be quite a success in the fall, with which they were delighted. The women sowed flax wherever they could dig a place to grow it. This entailed a lot of work. In the fall they cut it and had to beat it with a flail used for threshing by hand, which they called "scutching", to separate the woody fibers from the valuable fiber, to spin and weave into bedding, tablecloth and towels. They bartered fish to get a couple of sheep. They sheared the wool, carded it by hand into rolls to spin and weave into cloth, as no woman would be without a spinning wheel, which would be a disgrace!

There was a wonderful community spirit in those days. They had social gatherings for work, and entertainment such as quilting bees, spinning frolics to spin the yarn for knitting and weaving. Then came the thickening frolics where they dampened the cloth when taken out of the loom, put it on a large table and kneaded back and forth until the right thickness was attained. There would be four women on each side of the table doing this and singing Gaelic songs. The thick part of the cloth was called drugget and was used for making men's pants and women's skirts.

My grandmother had six more children, all born at home attended by a midwife. As there was no school at High Bank, one son and two neighbor boys walked from High Bank to Uigg to go to school there, a distance of approximately thirteen miles. There the boys worked for their board in homes where they stayed from

Monday to Friday. Those three boys and one from Orwell later went to Prince of Wales College and graduated with honors. The four boarded together in Charlottetown, and all climbed the ladder of success. One was knighted, one a judge in La Mesa, California, one a mayor of Bismarck, North Dakota, and the fourth an associate professor in Michigan. I am sure the mothers of all those boys played a most important part in the successes and 'mother's prayers' followed them throughout their lives. All the mothers worked happily to raise their families in Christian homes where Sunday and mid-week services were held weekly.

My mother's life was very different. Roads were opened up everywhere. Post Offices were few and far between in her teen-age years. Mail was taken to Vernon River from Murray Harbor by a man on horseback. He met the mail from Charlottetown, and residents received mail once or twice a week. Schools were opened in each district, also gristmills where flour and oatmeal were ground. Tanneries where leather was tanned for shoes, harness etc. She saw mills, blacksmith shops and stores. Fifty to one hundred acres were cleared and good crops raised with plenty of feed for the horses, cows, sheep and hogs. Comfortable homes were built and heated with high oven stoves, 'Old Yarmouth' and 'Waterloo' were the ones that I heard most about. Baking and cooking was much easier and kerosene and Aladdin Lamps replaced candles. Grandmother's old wooden wash tub was replaced with galvanized ones. Wells were dug at every home. Water was raised in a large bucket by a rope fastened to a wooden drum called a windlass upon which the hoisting rope was turned by means of winding by hand. Iron sinks drained their water by pipes to a compost pile of earth out in the field quite some distance from the house.

Beautiful sets of dishes could be purchased and also nice enamel cooking utensils. Mother said Grandma loved pretty dishes and this has followed down all along the line as that still is the first place I go to in a store, my daughters and granddaughters seem to have the same interest. Mother said they used steel knives and forks in her younger days and it was her job to keep them polished with fine white sand that could be found in certain fields. In the fall they would fill a big crock with the sand so as not to run out of it through the winter. Women in this era did a lot of spinning, weaving, knitting and sewing. Mother liked to paint pictures, crochet and embroider. She learned tailoring in Boston, men and women's suits were what she specialized in. She always enjoyed sewing. I did not, especially after I made a suit for myself and she made me take a sleeve out nine times before it met her approval. She would hook from four to nine lovely hand stamped mats in a winter. She made a lot of her dyes from moss and leaves, but diamond dyes made less work in matching colors.

My life was similar to my mother's in respect to the work we did, only every year seemed to bring something new to all. Seeing the first train come to Murray Harbor was quite a thrill. We had trains going to Charlottetown six days a week, and post offices in most districts delivering mail six days a week. Saturdays were always express days. On freight days it was quite a tiresome trip as there would be so much shunting of the cars back and forth. The train was nick named 'The Gaelic Express'. Later, we had a good bus service, now we have neither to depend on. .

I was very lucky in 1909 when my parents gave me an organ. Having musical neighbors, they came in very often especially on Sunday nights and sung all those old gospel hymns. On weeknights they came with a bass viol., auto harps and a flute. So I was brought up to be really fond of singing and music. So many things were developed for convenience, such as the telephone. Radio made hard work easier when one could relax and hear nice music and news from different parts of the world, although during the war, it was very depressing and sad too. The coming of electricity to our area in 1950 brightened our homes and store and the electric washing machines saved a lot of time over the hand operated machines. Now we had bathrooms, hot and cold water in the taps, and many other gadgets. Wages were very low, but it seemed so rewarding to work hard for things we needed. We always had plenty to eat and to give away. We raised our own beef, pork, lamb and chickens. Can anyone imagine having a 300 lb carcass of beef *hanging in an outbuilding now, as we used to do, and have no need for a lock on the door! I canned meat, soup, haddock, clams, quahogs, lobster, cherries, strawberries, plums as well as making many quarts of preserves of all kinds and pints of jelly, jams and pickles. We had our own milk, cream, butter and buttermilk and I baked all the bread, rolls, biscuits, pies, cakes, cookies that appeared on our table.*

Doctors drove many miles on stormy winter nights to relieve suffering and sometimes to take a patient to hospital. This is not done now, any more than having a midwife for a confinement case.

Labor saving devices have spared my daughters from heavy work, but sometimes it seems to me that they are under more pressure than the women of my generation. When my grandchildren were growing up they attended different schools, had music lessons in different places, sports and church groups that they had to be taken to. It seemed as though, even with public transportation, their mothers spent half their time in the car driving one child or the other somewhere. Education was more accessible when they were growing up and in the past few years wages have been raised that enables them to travel to many parts of the world and is really an education in itself. My married granddaughters start life on their wedding day with more beautiful things, new cars, homes, furniture, electrical appliances, etc., than my grandmother ever saw. Yet every generation has its share of both hardships and happiness, and no doubt over the years they too will see changes. My opinion on life is what you make it. Trust in God and he will direct our paths."

Some News Snippets

Colonial Herald, Jan. 5, 1839

'*Last evening, Mr. William Irving, Jr., of Cherry Valley was unfortunately drowned near Second Creek, within a mile & a half of his residence. He was on his return from town, accompanied by his wife & another female, by the same track he had* taken in the morning, when his horse fell through the ice. By his assistance, the 2 females were got safely out of the sleigh, but in attempting to extricate the horse, he fell in himself, & his body was not discovered until this morning, when it was found under the horse.'

Colonial Herald, Feb. 15, 1840.

'LAUNCHED on the 6th inst. from the ship yard of Messers. McCallum & Gregor, Brackley Point, a superior built Schooner of 190 tons, called the CHARLES. She was hauled on the ice to the channel, nearly a quarter of a mile, by forty pair of horses.'

Royal Gazette March 22, 1842

'Last evening a poor man named Alexander Nicholson from the Big Woods, Murray Harbour Road Settlement, about 4 weeks since he was in the woods chopping a log, which resting on the branches, after a second gave way, turned over on his leg, & a snag taking hold of his flesh, tore it off down to his foot, & completely dislocated his knee. His mother & his wife being the only persons near at the time, got him home & there being no medical assistance in the Settlement, he continued to linger for some days, when he was brought to town, but it was too late to render him any assistance. He suffered the most excruciating pains from 10 o'clock yesterday morning until 10 at night when he expired. His wife has since been delivered of twin children, & her life is despaired of. The deceased came to the Island 2 years ago, from the Isle of Sky, & is 29 years of age.'

Royal Gazette, Charlottetown, July 15, 1845

'Another distressing accident occurred at Big Cape, Lot 42 on Friday last. Angus Macdonald of that place with his four sons, and a son of John Macintyre, a lad of about 14 years of age, and a son of Donald Macdonald went out a-fishing. In the afternoon the wind veered round from the North to the South, *which caused a high sea which upset the boat, and they were all thrown overboard. After struggling for some time, in the water, they were all drowned except one of the sons of Angus Macdonald, who was washed on shore, where he was found in a state of insensibility. He was put into a cart and taken home, and now lies in a precarious state. Four other bodies have since been found.'*

Mail Boats on the Ice

'Long before the Confederation Bridge, and before the institution of regular year round ferry service, ice boats served the Island's mail service and passenger needs during the long winter months. The Cape service was instituted in 1827 when Donald McInniss and Neil Campbell crossed from P.E.I. to Cape Tormentine, New Brunswick demonstrating the feasibility of this crossing. In 1829 the government entered into an agreement to begin the service on a regular basis.

The ice boats were small (5 m. long, 2 m. wide avg.), and made as light as possible while maintaining their strength. They were equipped with runners on each side of the hull to allow them to be dragged across the ice-flows and snow. Straps attached to the boats and to the crew, allowed them to haul the boat, and acted as a safety harness should they break through the ice. Many accidents happened over the years.'

CHAPTER 12

Residents of Camustianavaig

"Thigeadh bochdainn no bearteas,

Thigeadh acaid no leòn,

Chaoidh cha sgar iad mo chuimhne

Bho na glinn sin ri m'bheo;

Ged a shiubhlainn gach riogh-achd

Is gach tir fo na neòil,

Bidh mo chridhe gu deireadh

Ann an Eilean a' cheò."

" Come poverty or riches,

Come grief or wound,

Never will they sever my memory

From these glens where I live;

Though I were to traverse

Every kingdom under the sun,

My heart will be forever

In the Island of the Mist."

Neil MacLeod (Niall Dhòmhaill nan Òran)

We have observed in Chapter 10 that the Camustianavaig township was separated into twelve crofts after John Blackadder's 1811 survey of Clan MacDonald Estate. In the superb Clan Donald Centre and Museum of the Isles at Armadale in south Skye the public can get access to lots of information in the rent records from 1823 onwards.

The tenants of the twelve Camustianavaig Crofts in 1823, with a total acerage of 57.944 'arable', plus a total of 1024.322 acres pasture were:-

1	Archibald MacLean	2	Donald Matheson
3	Donald MacLean	4	Murdo MacLeod
5	Alexander MacKenzie	6	*John Campbell
7	*Alexander Campbell	8	*Neil Campbell
9	John MacDonald	10	Alexander Nicolson
11	Alexander MacLeod	12	Murdo MacKinnon

*Born in Snizort Parish. Were they 3 brothers perhaps?

With such 'deliberately' tiny patches of land to cultivate, in this and other Braes townships, it is no wonder that Alexander Stewart, an emigrant from Peinchorran, Braes, who had purchased 100 acres of land in Prince Edward Island, wrote the following to his family in Skye in 1815.

*"Dear Father you said if I would send you good news that you would all come. I have no news to send but this, that I think it better for one to work for himself and ripe(reap) the benifit of it, than work for others and be sent off after all their labor. There is plenty of lands here wood lands from 15/- per acre to 2/6 & clear lands from £1-10 to £1 per acre & liced (leased) lands from 1/- to/6 per acre and the lice 999 years and farms that they give upon halfs the owner of the lands provide cattle and sheep & seed for sowing & receives the one half of all the produce. My advice would be to you or any other that comes out that they should take care of their money. I would that everyone should keep their own & then they can take lands or anything that they can see to their best advantage. It would be best for a family to pay for their passage and find their own victuals, only the Cap't to find them in water, for ship allowance is very dry & another thing if any of it remains they can take it with them - especially barley which is not be had here... You wanted to let you know how I live in the woods, I live better than ever I did in Scotland off Tea & sugar. Beef, Mutton & Pork would serve & Rum three times in the day.
Your affectionate son,
Alex."*

The particular Camustianavaig crofts which are of interest to us are Nos. 4, 6, 8 and 11.

No. 6 was occupied by John Campbell, writer of Letter 3, who was a brother of Effy's mother, Chirsty. She was married to Effy's dad, Hugh Macdonald. They lived at No. 8 from 1830. It is evident from comments made in Letter 3, that Hugh took over the tenancy of this croft from the Alexander Campbell who was Murdoch's host in Scotch Settlement, PEI and Effy's cousin. It is likely they sailed together in 1830. In 1833 the tenancy of croft 11 went to John Macdonald Jr., son of Hugh Macdonald (i.e. he was Effy's brother). The former tenant was an Alexander MacLeod. He is not Murdoch's brother Alastair Beag (born 1810), as this person was already tenant here in 1823. Alastair Beag would have been only 13 years old then.

The 'MacLeods of PEI' book says that Murdoch's father was also named Murdoch. Could he be the tenant of No. 4 in 1823? If so we have a problem, as from 1826 to 1829, the tenancy is shown as 'Murdo MacLeod's heirs'. Had he died? If so, this cannot be our Murdoch's dad as the letters refer to him as being alive in Camustianavaig in 1832 and in PEI in 1838. Perhaps he was incapacitated and had voluntarily passed the tenancy to other family members – Letter 2 mentions that he had been ill. By 1830 the tenancy is in the names of 'Rory MacLeod and mother'. Mother's name is dropped after 1834 – had she died or could she and her husband have emigrated?

My own theory is that Murdoch's father was not a Murdoch MacLeod at all, but an Alexander MacLeod, very likely the tenant of croft 11 who left before 1833. This is of course speculation – we have no hard facts to go on. It is unfortunate that the rent records only give the name of the croft tenant. We have to wait until 1841 for the names of individuals in the Government Census, and by then our families have emigrated. None the less, the census data is interesting for these particular crofts and it also tells us that eight cottar (landless) families had built houses in the township, presumably with the consent of the estate proprietors.

Croft 4	Croft 6	Croft 8	Croft 11
Rory MacLeod 50	John Campbell 55	Hugh Macdonald75	John Macdonald35
Catherine Do. 50	Mary 45	Chirsty Do. 60	Ann Do. 25
Donald Do. 25	Christina Do. 25	Arch. Do. 30	James Do. 5
Mary Do. 25	Jessie Do. 20	Ann Do. 25	Hugh Do. 4
William Ross 12	Malcolm Do. 15	Mary Do. 20	Malcolm Do. 2
	Ann Do. 15	Duncan MacKay30	Alex MacQueen 15
	Alex. Do. 13	Alex Do. 3	
	John Do. 10	Samuel MacLeod20	
	Jessie Nicolson 1		

CHAPTER 13

Interpreting the Letters

Using the data available to me from the Old Parish Registers of Portree, Government Census information from both Skye and PEI and the help of my e-mail correspondents, I have attempted to interpret the letters from Camustianavaig.

In order to make it easier for the reader, I have used numerical superscripts, for example [1] [2] etc. These then appear as notes for each letter in the right-hand column.

Letter 1.
Effy MacDonald to Murdoch MacLeod

[Envelope]

Mr Murdoch MacLeod

Squire Wright*

Prince Town Road

16 miles from Charlotte Town

Prince Edward Island

North America

[postmark May 20 1831]

Thomas Wright was an early colonial surveyor who lived and worked in Prince Edward Island. This resulted in his descendants being one of the longest established English families in the Province. (The Wrights of Middleton).

*Squire Wright is probably Charles Wright, a member of this family, who was himself a landlord, but also attorney for Louisa Augusta Fanning, Lady Wood, who was the major landowner in lot 67. (see Chapter 9)

Murdoch probably worked as an estate joiner on behalf of the squire.

[The first fragment is missing ....then.....]

.....Iain Campbell[1]: a bed; twenty barrels of seed

1. It is difficult to tell what was in the missing fragment and which particular Iain Campbell is referred to, but it is unlikely to be the John Campbell mentioned later (Iain is the Gaelic form for John) as he was established in croft 6 Camustianavaig from at least 1823.

....from Benifiler[2] [Penifiler]

2. Penifiler is a neighbouring township to Camustianavaig. Until 1831 the tacksman tenant was Captain Alexander MacLeod, a veteran of the Napoleonic Wars. He built Mossbank House in 1782. Alexander retained three arable parks and continued to reside there after the township was crofted. There is no evidence that he was a relative of Murdoch. We know that several families moved, as cottars (landless), to Camustianavaig from An Gorstan (near Penifiler) in the early 1830s.

they themselves have now sold the place and given it up[3].

3. Penifiler was first crofted in 1831, so the reference to 'giving up the place' is more likely to refer to one of the Camustianavaig crofts which had been crofted since 1811.

I took it before I got your letter and I'm resolved to work the croft[4]. Along with that the autumn was wet, we had a lot of snow and frost over the winter and we're having a wet spring. You'll be planting for us, if you are wanting us after writing this letter.

Iain Breabadair (the weaver) from Raasay, was saying in my house that he himself and his sons are with MacKenzie[5] who used to be signing people up. He got 27 families at the first meeting in Raasay. They are going over after May market in 2 ships. Tell what extra trouble there is between getting your letter and our letter. I don't have ___ [time] to put more in it but my thousand ____ [blessings] to yourself, lad, and tell will I give more school to go a distance for

4. Croft 8 at Camustianavaig was vacated by Alexander Camp-bell in 1830. Did he sail with Murdoch? According to the rent books, Effy's father Hugh Macdonald became tenant. As he would have been 65 years old at the time, perhaps Effy and her 20 year old brother Archie took charge of the croft work. Or was Effy working Murdoch's father's croft 4 or croft 11? Letter 2 says she was not living wife Murdoch's parents.

5. MacKenzie was the emigration agent. ("used to be signing people up", idiomatic Gaelic for "is in the habit of …")

6. This Alasdair is very likely Alexander Campbell, son of Neil Campbell, previously of croft 8, with whom Murdoch lodged in Scotch Settlement. With Brian Cox's help, we now think that Alexander Campbell, married to Flora MacSween or MacSwain, lived in the Hunter River area, at Malpeque Road in Lot 23. From the baptismal records of their children (baptised by Rev. John MacLennan) we know that he and his wife emigrated before

any sense whatever that is in us. Give our blessings all together to Alasdair[6] and his people and how good they have been to you and Alasdair is useful in sending news.

1836 and that his date of birth was about 1810. There is however another Alexander Campbell who lived in this area. His death notice in 1855, age 80, specifically says 'came 1830 from Skye'. In Skye, the use of *sloinneadh* (patronymics) would have made it much easier to distinguish between individuals of the same name. For example: I am *Iain, Sheorais, Shomhairle, Sheorais, Iain, Thoramaid* (Ian, son of George, son of Samuel, son of George, son of John, son of Norman). It is almost certain that the same system was continued in PEI but not, unfortunately, in official documents!

Norman[7] is sending his kind compliments to you Murdoch and to his sisters and brothers. You yourself know that I was most desirous of going there, as there was not any trade whatsoever going on. I was obliged to get married and there is no regret whatever on me but to be missing my sisters and brothers.

7. Probably Norman Campbell, Murdoch's friend (see letter 2). He may have been a relative of Alexander's. The suggestion is that all his siblings had gone to PEI. Brian has discovered that Norman and his wife Anna MacLean(!) later lived very close to Alexander in Lot 23 PEI. He emigrated in 1840/41. In the 1881 census for Lot 23 we have a Neil Campbell 1806-1889 born Scotland, Hugh Campbell 1829-1901 born PEI,

Mary Campbell 1827-1911 born PEI and Catherine Campbell 1819-1901 born PEI, four brothers and sisters. Their parents were John Campbell c1780-? And Mary nee MacKinnon 1787-1878. Could these be Norman's brothers and sisters. Was this John his father and was Mary his stepmother? (see letter 2). John, Mary and young Neil must have emigrated before 1819 if Catherine's DOB is correct!

I was advised by my mother's brother John Campbell[8] and it was around August Fair I did it[9].

8. John Campbell of croft 6 was Effy's mother Chirsty's brother and the writer of letter 3.

9. *"In 1580 a licence was obtained from the crown for the institution of a fair at Portree. This market was held twice a year from Wednesday to Saturday when the various products of the island were exposed for sale – meal, butter, cheese, poultry, sheep, cattle and horses, hides, wool, linen, and dried fish, especially herrings and salmon."* Alexander Nicolson, 'History of Skye'. What was the 'it' that Effy did?

It's from Anna MacLean[10] that I have got three parts of all what he[11] had and half of the boat and nets. Iain Campbell[12] is saying that what I got went for 35 pounds and you tell me or will any other worry come on me which of them is better for me to go or stay with your father and I am putting my [?? unclear]

it would be worse than going if you consider your father[13] that it would be better for me to go than to stay at the way that I have considering my situation. Write to me as you said since I'm telling you where I am and _____ I expect to build a house and since you _____ on me I won't build it until I get your letter. Anna is sending her blessings and to all the relations and to your own self Murdoch.

10. The 2 Ann MacLeans in the 1841 Census for Camustianavaig would have been too young in 1831. Archie MacLean, 60 year old crofter at croft 1 seems to be a widower in 1841. Perhaps his deceased wife was Anna MacLean? A much more likely suggestion comes from Brian Cox. Norman Campbell of Hunter River PEI (Lot 23) is married to an Anna MacLean (b. 1813). They emigrated 1840/41 with son Donald (b. 1840 at Portree).

11. Who was he? Possibly a deceased person. A relative of Anna's?

12. The Iain Campbell mentioned at 1 perhaps? It is interesting that she makes a distinction between John Campbell and Iain Campbell but, as now, some men were known by the Gaelic version of their name and some by the English version.

13. The suggestion here is that Murdoch's father required assistance in some way from Effy. Was he disabled or ill?

Send word to my godfather(?) (The Gaelic word goisdeidh can be used as a term of endearment), Roderick(?) and tell him that his people expect him to send them a letter and I myself would like to get word about him[14]. Your mother[15] is sending blessings with added good wishes to you indeed, and I will be glad to see you, if you wish, and everybody at Alasdair's as well.

14. It is impossible to tell who this is. The only Roderick I've come across is one of the four sons of Ludvik MacIntosh. His widow was still alive at the 1895 Strathalbyn Jubilee.

15. This is the first indication that Murdoch's mum is also alive.

Letter 2
Effy MacDonald to Murdoch MacLeod

[Envelope]
    Mr. Murdoch MacLeod, Esq.
    Care of Alex'd [Alexander] Campbell
    Malpeque Road
    Prince Edw Islan
    [post marked Portree, 1832]

Camastianavaig 23rd May 1832

Dear Murdo,

I received your letter and I am very glad to hear you are in good health and prospering so well in the world, and this is to inform you that I am in good health at present, thanks God for it. Hoping this will find you in the same.

I have heard you are going to marry & if you think that expedient and lawful for yourself to do you may do it for I hope I'll never trouble you for it for I have none to take care of in this cause but myself and I hope by God's grace I shall keep myself chaste and virtuous tho' you should prove so perfidious as to forget the name of Effy Macdonald and attach yourself to another but if you do that God grant her a better usage than I got and may He never impute to you as a crime my sufferings; at His judgement seat[1].

You are getting strange news from your Friend, but I think the friend is a good inventor of lies. He told you in his

1. Historical sources tell us that it was not unusual for husbands who had emigrated to North America without their wives, to simply abandon them in this way and marry another ("irregular marriage" by cohabitation and repute was acceptable under Scots Law). Effy evidently feared the worst.

letters that I burnt the letter you sent me from Tobermory[2], but you need not believe that. It is like every other adious [sic, odious] news you hear about me and my relatives for I have the letter carefully in my vest as dry as my silk handkerchief. I would not burn a letter from a more inconsiderate person in my esteem than you. I declined sending it in this letter to you for fear of putting you to expenses but I'll send it by some emigrant from this to that Island this year to let you see the malevolence your friend bears to me in giving you such an account of me and my relations. You heard that I did not visit your father while laying sick. By witness of some of my neighbours I was there several times but there were some persons in who would not say a Single word to me since my going in till I went out again tho' it was not your father or mother[3].

They are all now intending to emigrate to that country being prepared for it having roped [sic, rouped]

2. The emigrant ship had its last port of call at Tobermory before crossing the Atlantic.

3. Effy had been the subject of malicious gossip and false information had been conveyed to Murdoch. Was this as a result of jealousy? This also indicates that she was not living with Murdoch's parents, which was a choice she was considering in letter 1.

all their goods and furniture and set off the land. You were saying in the late letter you sent me that you would not believe anything I would say in my own justification unless you father was witness of it. Your father is now going and you shall learn of him how things are at present[4]. You were grieved at my sending you an unlocked letter before but you must excuse me it was not my fault for I delivered the unlocked letter to Norman Campbell[5] and he promised me he would lock it. I was newly delivered[6] as I told you and was unable to go anywhere for wafer and wax to lock it. What you shall have [unclear word follows] that what was spoken of my [unclear words] is to write shortly himself and he says he is much obliged to you for letting him know it.

But is not my business to the answering for such[7]. You must excuse me for the direction [postal address in PEI] as yourself did not let me know how to direct to you.

4. From 1833 the tenancy of croft 4 is in the name of Roderick MacLeod but had previously been tenanted by Murdo MacLeod's heirs. If this was our Murdoch's father something does not fit. Alternatively John Macdonald, son of Hugh MacDonald, i.e. Effy's brother, becomes the new tenant of No. 11 in 1833, when it was vacated by Alexander MacLeod. Was Alexander, Murdoch's father?

5. Norman Campbell as in letter 1.

6. The birth of one of Murdoch and Effy's children born nine months after dad's departure.

7. Norman Campbell's explanation presumably.

My compliments to yourself and to my uncle and aunt[8]. My mother and all the family sends their compliments to the same and begs them to write to them as soon as you deliver their compliments and are greatly surprised that they got no news of [them] before this.

My compliments to Alex'd [Alexander] Campbell and am much obliged for declaring he would be my friend[9] if I should go there but he has as many thanks as though I would trouble him. I desired the little boy [Murdoch and Effy's son Murdoch (Jr)] to send you his compliments. The boy said he would do it tomorrow & he expects every day to sail in a little boat to see yourself and he'll not bring his grandfather[10] lest he drink too much of the whisky on the way. Norman Campbell does not intend to go at all he is building a new house[11] [and] he [is] in good health and sending

8. Possibly Neil Campbell and his wife, former crofter of No. 8. They may well be Alexander Campbell's parents. If so they probably emigrated earlier than Murdoch's group along with Norman's parents and siblings: or were Norman's parents, John Campbell and his wife Mary, nee MacKinnon, Effy's aunt and uncle? I'm becoming increasingly attracted to the latter suggestion. The rent book shows Alexander taking over croft 8 from his father in 1826. Is it not more likely that Neil had died? My overall impression is that Murdoch's host in PEI is an older man, is he the Alexander Campbell born 1785. (see letter1)

9. Sponsor.

10. Probably Hugh Macdonald, Effy's father, as there is a suggestion in letter 3 that he may like to imbibe!

his compliments to his father[12], stepmother, brothers and sisters.

      I am your affectionate Wife

Effy MacDonald

11. There is no indication that Norman Campbell built a new house. The only Norman Campbell in Portree Parish at the 1841 Census is a farrier, living in a lodging house in Portree. The suggestion that he had also emigrated to PEI is very likely (see letter 1).

12. Very likely John and Mary Campbell and their two sons and two daughters (see letter 1).

Letter 3

John Campbell to Murdoch MacLeod

[Envelope]
Mr. Murdo MacLeod
Squire Wright Lot 67 Anderson1 Road
Scotch Settlement
Prince Edwaed's Island (sic)
North America
[post marked 17 ? 1838]

Camastianavaig, Portree Parish 13 August 1838,

Dear Murdo,

Your letter dated the 16th Dec'r 1837 came to my hands in Spring and I don't doubt you are a little surprised for my being so long silent but you need not, because I was willing that people might evancine [evince?] themselves, and that I would examine them too but that was of no effect[2]. Effy your wife is anxious of reaching you as any wife on earth could be but what can the wishes of a woman do when she has no means to assist her, she has nothing in the world and her father Hugh is the very Hugh you have seen yourself there is no alteration and therefore she is unable to do

1. Anderson Road, named after a Scottish Pioneer and opened in 1833-34.

2. Having received mixed messages about his wife and family, Murdoch has written to a trusted friend in the Camustianavaig community.

anything in going where you are unless you do it for yourself[3]. Therefore my opinion and advice to you if you regard your wife or children is to send for them immediately because they are very well worthy of any trouble you can take for them, because the children would be a grace and delight to many a prince in a palace, they are in good health and is present with me this very moment, if you are anxious of getting your wife and children as I take you to be I do not know what will detain you but you must come yourself personally or else send a check on the national bank office at Portree to put money to any friend on whom you would depend to act for you and likewise instructions and directions to her on her arrival what to do and who to find you out the above you must send to me or some other friend and if not, you need not be troubling yourself upon the subject. Minds your son is not in the mean time in but while he was in school he

3. Although Murdoch's parents have emigrated to PEI, Effy and their children have not gone. The reason is that she cannot raise the fare.

was very good to learn but is not able to sign his name there is no school this side of Portree so as poor people cannot reach at it[4]. You must not be blaming Effy if she was as able to reach you as I understand you are to reach her there is a long time since she had gone. Murdo I was very much surprised that you did not mention any thing concerning that colony and my old acquaintances and especially your father[5]. But although not I shall acquaint you of some of the country news in the first place. I have to let you know that I am in good health but my wife is always poorly. There is a mineral well or fountain found in Stenshal[6] in the Eastside of Trotternish

4. The SPCK schools tended to be temporary in the townships. It was a 4 mile walk to the Portree school.

5. Proof that Murdoch's father had emigrated.

6. This is *Loch Seunta* (the Loch of Enchantment) in the Parish of Stenschol, Trotternish. It is said to be fed by springs called *Tobar na Beatha* (the Well of Life), *Tobar na Slàinte* (the Well of Health) and *Tobar an Dòchas* (the Well of Hope). It had the reputation of being a place of healing. In Victorian

such as that one that is in Dingwall[7] which is of great comfort to many and my wife is there at present. The oldest of my daughters married and is very well off but Marion had the misfortune of losing her husband, and she is married again the second time. Chirsty[8] my youngest by the first wife is likewise on the point of marrying,

Jessy[9] the oldest by the second wife[10] is in Portree in the Sewing School and she is a fine girl. Malcolm and Alexander is likewise in Portree School. Malcolm is learning the Latin language since two or three years past and on the three last examinations of the school he has gained the prize and Sandy is getting on very well too and John the youngest boy is in school.

times it became particularly popular and 'prayer rags' were hung on the hazel trees around the loch margins. Invalids came to bathe in the waters and it was reckoned a crime to take a trout from the sacred pool.

7. The healing waters at Strathpeffer, a spa town, near Dingwall, Ross-shire.

8. Chirsty or Kirsty Campbell married Donald MacLeod, son of Roderick and Marsily MacLeod of croft 4. Her mother, John Campbell's fist wife was Janet Matheson.

9. Jessie age 20 is at her parents' home in 1841.

10. John's 2nd wife Mary, (nee Nicolson according to the marriage certificate and daughter Ann's birth in 1826 but MacKay at the births of Malcolm, Alexander and John, so she had probably been earlier widowed), is still alive in 1841 but by 1851 John is a widower (They had married on January 1st 1820). In the 1861 Census, John, age 77 has remarried.

His third wife was my great-grandmother Flora, nee MacQueen (they married on 19th June 1854). Flora was the widow of my great-grandfather John Macdonald who died in 1847.

I have to let you know that I got a letter from a friend of mine from New South Wales Australia one Charles Campbell[11]

11. "Friend" was often used in Gaelic for "relative". Could this Charles Campbell be a **very** famous one? Born 1810 – Died 1888, pastoralist and politician of New South Wales, third son of Robert Campbell, merchant of Campbell's Wharf Sydney. Charles was a precocious child and was taught by classical tutors before attending the famous schools of Thomas Reddall and Rev. Wilkinson. Afterwards he studied in Europe but decided on a country life. Finding that, except for a few convicts, labour for his huge sheep enterprise was scarce, he provided funds for Scottish shepherds to get passage to Australia. He arranged for others to come out in ships trading for Campbell and

Co. Among these was Angus MacMillan (1810-1865), a native of Skye, who made a remarkable journey in search of pastureland. "In 1840, accompanied only by aboriginal guides, and using a compass and a primitive chart, he discovered 'beautiful rich open plains', which he called Caledonia Australis." Another Skye shepherd, John MacKinnon aged 62, wrote home about his good fortune in Australia; *"I have in my possession this night, after clearing all expenses, twenty pounds sterling ... How long I would be in Skye before I would gather so much! ... When I came ashore I had only 10/-."*

This Charles Campbell evidently had great faith in the Highlanders. In 1870 he was nominated for the Australian Legislative Council and took an active part in its debates. He returned to Scotland, however, and died in Inverness in 1888.

That this is the same Charles Campbell is pure speculation, but I would **love** it to be true!

to send Malcolm[12] to himself because he has made a fortune there but I think I shall not [unclear line but appears to be "send him there four years"].

You may tell your father and my friend Alex'd Campbell[13] if they have done well for themselves they have done exceedingly for Hugh and his children because they are the only men here now.

12. It is interesting that Malcolm, the Latin scholar with such prospects, did **not** emigrate to Australia or indeed anywhere else. In the Census of 1861 he is a farmer of **4 acres** at Conordan! His son John went on to tenant Glenvaragill Farm near Portree and his daughter Mary married Rev Ewen MacQueen of Camustianavaig, minister at Inverness.

Malcolm's brothers Alexander and John and his sisters Ann and Jessie did all however take passage to Australia on the ship 'Arabian' in 1854 along with several families from Camustianavaig, Conordan and Achnahanaid.

13. Hugh Macdonald took over croft 8, formerly tenanted by an Alexander Campbell. Hugh's son John took over croft 11, formerly tenanted by an Alexander MacLeod. None of Hugh's family have any connection with croft 4, formerly tenanted by a Murdo MacLeod's heirs.

They built a storehouse and they now fish curens[14] [?] buying herrings and freighting vessels,

you can tell your father that Donald Kennedy[15] failed in Upper Ollach and that the farm was offered to me and I refused it and that because I would only get a lace [lease] of five years only, I was afraid if I would be turned out at the end of the five year I would not get as good a chance as what I had.

This leads me to the conclusion that our Murdoch's father is more likely to be Alexander MacLeod of croft 11. The Macdonalds were very much involved in the fishing trade, which may have been the province of MacLeod and Campbell previously.

14. 'Frail boats?, perhaps dinghies'. They fished close to shore with nets.

15. Donald Kennedy is shown as tenant of the Upper Ollach farm in 1830, Lieutenant John MacLeod's heirs relinquished it in 1829. In the 1841 Census there are no Donald Kennedys in north Skye and there is evidence that he had died before then. He had married for the third time in 1827 to a Catherine Kelly. She is found in the 1841 Census in Screapadal, Raasay with John, Jean and Catherine, Donald's children from his marriage to Isabel MacQueen plus her own children. We also find a

Time would fail me in telling you all I would wish. Peter Beaton[16] and his family is just as you have seen them.

Angus Nicholson Drumaoish [Drumuie][17] has four boys and Samuel his brother is lying idle not doing a turn for a long time past,

your Uncles daughter and her mother[18] is in the old condition.

James Kennedy (Donald's eldest son) with his wife and baby daughter, in the same township. Brian Cox believes they were his great-great-grand aunt and uncle.

16. The only Peter Beatons in the area in the 1841 Census is a 20 year old mariner, living in Portree and an agricultural labourer, also 20, living in Snizort. Neither appear to be married men. Our Peter Beaton seems to have left the area.

17. He and his wife Susana (sic) have four boys in 1841 and a little girl, Effie, has been added to the family. He is indeed living in Drumuie, near Portree. There is however, no Samuel Nicolson, other than a child, living in the area. Has he emigrated?

18. It has not been possible to determine who these may be, but, in 1841 there is a 12 year old Jessie MacLeod living with a 30 year old Mary MacLeod in Conordon. Mary is described as a pauper.

Is she a widow, or has Murdoch's uncle emigrated, leaving his wife and daughter?

Kenneth[19] your friend is still a bachelor for this time a twelve month was a very severe time and this summer was so with some too, but we have a fine appearance of crops this year and good price of cattle, but through all the dearth that was in the country I did not buy a grain. I have no more to add, Effy is present during the whole time. I am writing in the hopes of fulfilling of your former promises and matrimony vows to her and the presence of the Almighty God who will judge you and her and the presence of men also joins me with her love and best respects to you.

    I am your sincere friend and best wishes.

John Campbell.

PS

    I was on the point of forgetting that that I made your certificate[20] publickly known in all companies and places in which I happen to be and likewise thank you for forwarding it.

John Campbell.

19. Again difficult to be certain, but, in 1841 Kenneth MacLeod age 40, crofter of No. 4 Penifiler and a bachelor, seems to be the most likely.

20. Perhaps a certificate in connection with Murdoch's joinery trade or an advert for workers. He may have been a skilled house builder or good at teaching apprentices or he may have been a speciality carpenter. He obviously wished folk in Skye to be aware of him when emigrating.

Letter 4

Effy MacDonald to Murdoch MacLeod

[Envelope]:
   Mr. Murdoch MacLeod
   Prince Edward's Island
   Anderson Road Lot 67
   North America
   [post marked May W 27 N 1839]
   Camastianavaig 23rd May 1839

Dear husband

Your welcome letter came to
my hands yesterday evening
which gave me unspeakable
satisfaction to hear of your
welfare and the more so for
the contents it contained. I
have the pleasure of letting
you know that I and the children enjoys good health and
the boy is continually at
school, I was making all the
[unclear something like
arrangements] that was in my
power for emigrating since
Martinmass until a letter came
to Dugal MacPherson[1] from a
relation of his that is married
upon Alex'd Campbell's
daughter Mary which
contained that you sailed for
to come here in October last
and that discouraged me very
much [she was discouraged

1. There is a 20 year old
   Dougall MacPherson son
   of the farmer at Shulli-
   shadder, Portree, in the
   1841 Census.

because he never arrived, and she feared he may have been lost at sea], but now I revive and hope if the Almighty sees it proper to prosper with me I shall embrace the first opportunity of seeing you. There is to my opinion about 200 of the Raasay people for emigrating to that Island and if the Almighty spare me you may depend undoubtly of my being along with them wherever place they [a line is missing here] certain as yet what time because they did not get a vessel yet but they disposed of all there subjects [belongings] and is making ready every day with all the speed they can, some of them were promising to do the best assistance they could with me, but I rather think they have enough to assist themselves[2]. Arch'bd My brother and Ann my sister both married last winter. Archy and a lad from Flendranes [more likely Kendram in Kilmuir parish] one MacKay[3] bartered the one married the other's sister.

2. It seems that Effy's situation had become well known and she had the sympathy of the other potential emigrants.

3. In the 1841 Census, Ann Macdonald, age 25, is married to Donald MacKay, age 30, and they had a 3 year old son Alexander. All of these are living with Hugh Macdonald, age 75, and his wife Chirsty, age 60, plus a 20 year old Samuel MacLeod (joiner son of Roderick and Marsily MacLeod of croft 4), in the house on croft 8 Camustianavaig. Archie, age 30, although married to Ann MacKay, age 20, is also living with his parents. Surprisingly, Ann with their daughter

Tho as I have the intention of going I will not add any more but conclude with my best respects to you your children is present in the mean time and joins me with the same.

I remain you ever Loving Wife

Effy MacDonald
or MacLeod

Effie, age 2 (probably named for our Effy, her aunt), and a one month old baby girl (as yet unnamed) are living with Ann's parents, Kenneth and Margaret MacKay, at Kendram in the Kilmuir parish. Has she returned home to have her baby under mum's watchful eye, or has there been a domestic rift? In 1847 Archie is recorded as fathering a child with a Catherine MacInnes of Portree. Had he left his wife? Both mother and child, also named Catherine lived at Bayfield until the 1870s. Archie Macdonald and his wife Ann are nowhere to be found in the 1851 census or subsequently.

I, and several of those who have commented on the four letters have noticed that the one written by John Campbell seems much more 'literate' than those of Effy (particularly letters 1 and 2). One wonders if this is due to a difference in economic or social status between Effy and her uncle. Does it, more likely, show a difference in levels of education between male and female? Effy's letter 4 seems more in the style of Campbell's. Did Effy, perhaps get someone else to write this one?

CHAPTER 14

Reunion for Murdoch,
Effy and Family

"Gur mise bheir gradh gu brath do'n chailin

A dh' fhag mi sealan am dheidh;

Tha aice os chach gach agh 's gach barrachd,

Mar aille gealaich measg reul.

'S i seamh-osag fhann an t-samhraidh choibhneil

Bheir glean us coille fo bhlath;

'S le dubh-neoil a' gheamhraidh 's anrath gaillinn

Chan annsa fanail r' a sgath".

"I shall cherish forever a love for the girl whom I left behind me a short time ago; she possess a glory and virtue above all others, like the beauty of the moon among the stars. She is the light-winged breeze of gentle summer bringing warmth to glen and to forest; the dark clouds of winter and the gloom of the snow-storm will not linger when she is near."

Composed by Rev. James MacGregor, Cape Breton, but I'm sure the sentiments are those that Murdoch had for his Effy!

What have we discovered about Murdoch, Effy and their family?

The conclusion of **letter 4**, post-marked May 1839, leads us to anticipate that Effy and their children are preparing to sail west, their fare paid, either by Murdoch or by their relatives or sponsors.

The letters speak of Effy's *'children'* and *'the boy'*, from which we conclude that there was a boy and a girl........at least!

Now Murdoch MacLeod in its various forms, *'Murdock'*, *'Murdo'*, *'McLeod'*, *'M'leod'*, etc. was a very common name in Prince Edward Island in the mid 19th century, as was *'Effy'*, *'Effie'*, *'Euphemia'*, *'Phemie'* and *'Phebe'*: and so the task of 'Googling' the correct family proved challenging for me. During the 1830s Murdoch, *'the joiner'*, without family ties, seems to have been peripatetic and spent time in Lots 22, 23 as well as 67. In some of the letters he was *'care of Squire Wright'* and in some, *'care of Alexander Campbell'*, whom we believe to have been Effy's cousin. Many of the early PEI records were less than comprehensive and often only recorded family heads. So records of our Murdoch are difficult to identify with certainty.

One of the most obvious documents to consult is a book by Harold S. MacLeod, entitled, appropriately enough, *'The MacLeods of Prince Edward Island'*. At last we find something of interest on page 207.

"Murdock MacLeod, was born in Scotland c1807, the son of Murdock MacLeod. He married Phoebe MacDonald, 1808-1901. They spoke Gaelic. He left his wife and three children in Scotland and came to PEI with his two brothers Angus (**we have no futher trace of Angus unless he is the Angus McLeod who was a witness on 16th October 1860, at the marriage of Ann McLeod, our Murdoch's daughter.**) and Sandy around 1830. Nine years later he sent for his wife and three children: Murdock Jr., Ann, and Chirstie(1). They had five other children born in PEI. Margaret born in Strathalbyn, PEI, John born in Strathalbyn, Kate, ditto, Chirsty (2) ditto, (Chirstie (1) had died), (**NB this was a wrong assumption**), Donald born in Strathalbyn c 1839 or 1841."

[**Information supplied by George H. MacLeod of Kernersville, North Carolina, a descendant of Donald.**]

So the MacLeod book leads us to believe that the couple had had three children in Skye, the third probably born after Murdock's departure in 1830, as letter 2 refers to Effy being *'newly delivered'* when she sent letter 1 *'unlocked'* in the absence of *'wafer and wax to lock it'* on May 20th 1831.

But what a surprise to find that Murdoch and Effy also had five other children born in Prince Edward Island!

We now had some names to aid us in our continued search of the PEI archives, plus the very able assistance, by e-mail, of Brian Cox who is researching his MacLeod and Nicholson ancestors, who also came from Braes, Skye in 1841 and settled in Lot 67.

From his extensive files, Brian was able to find a copy of the death notice of Murdoch's brother Alexander (Sandy or Alistair Beag) McLeod, (the schoolmaster) in the 'Island Farmer' of Thursday 16th December, 1897.

'MCLEOD, - At Springton, Lot 67, on the 28th ult., Alexander McLeod, aged 87 years, a native of Portree, Isle of Skye, whence he came to this province in 1830.'

I had also found a similar notice in the 'Summerside Journal', 15th December, 1897.

'MACLEOD – Lot 67, November 28th, Alex MacLeod age 87 Native of Portree, Isle of Skye. Emigrated 1830.'

We were on the same lines!

Brian also notes that it would not be unusual for Alexander to be absent from the census returns. As a bachelor, he would not be listed in 1841 or 1851 as he was not a family head and was probably boarding with some other family. Also, teachers moved around a lot so he could have been in other Lots in 1881 and 1891, and so difficult to identify. (All PEI Census record for 1871, apart from Lots 34 & 36, have been lost.)

With Brian's help however, the following listing in the 1881 census on Lot 22 seems very likely!

"Alexander MCLEOD Male Scottish age 73 born Scotland Farmer Presbyterian
Catherine NICHOLSON Female Scottish age 60, born Scotland, Presbyterian
Catherine NICHOLSON Female Scottish age 8, born Prince Edward Island, Presbyterian"

Brian also discovered a Murdoch McLeod in Lot 22 in the 1841 census. His household shows 1 male, 1 female of 16 to 45 years (Murdoch and Effy) and 1 male and 4 females less than 16. We would expect 2 males and 2 females under 16 (Murdoch Jr., Donald, Ann and Chirstie (1)). Of the seven people in the house only one was not born in Scotland. If this is the correct household, the one not born in Scotland is Donald, born 1841, the new baby mis-identified as female by the census innumerator. But who is the other female? Perhaps, as was common, she was a lodger, a young relative or a household servant.

In the 1861 census there is a Murdoch MacLeod, family head, on Lot 67. Based on who his census neighbours were, he lived at a place called Glen Valley or Junction Road which is on the Lot 22/67 boundary.

Further painstaking research has failed to find any other detailed reference to our Murdoch Sn., but with the help of George Sanborn we have the following:-

"Estates Division, P.E.I. Supreme Court
ESTATE OF MURDOCH McLEOD, LOT 67
Will. McL-249
Murdoch MacLeod of Springton, Lot 67, joiner
- ten pounds each to Donald my son and Catherine my daughter

- five pounds to my daughter Margaret
- 27 pounds to my daughter Christy the Younger as well as one cow and two sheep
- to my son John 100 acres adjoining Lot 22 on the east, except that part of it lying south of the Junction Road, subject to the following conditions: within five years of my decease he is to pay the above-mentioned sums and legacies to Donald, Catherine, and Margaret, and also 17 pounds of the bequest to Christy the Younger; he shall also pay the children of my deceased daughter, Christy the Elder, five pounds as directed by my executor. He shall also pay 20 pounds to John Murdoch Vickerson, son of my deceased daughter, Ann, when he becomes 21 years of age. My son John shall also not sell the land unless he chooses to take a cash settlement instead of my bequest in which case he must signify the same in writing to my son
Murdoch. In that event, my son Murdoch is to pay John 100 pounds and take possession of the land as above, assuming all the above conditions.
- to my son John all my joiner's tools "including the cramp"
- my beloved wife Euphemia to be comfortably maintained during her natural life by my son Murdoch, she to live in his household unless she wants two separate rooms in his house
- Murdoch my son to be my executor and also to have all the rest of my real estate and personal estate, he to pay my daughter Christy the Younger within five years of my decease all that part of her bequest over and above what John in accepting the land should pay her, namely ten pounds cash, one cow and two sheep.
14 November 1871/s/ Murdoch MacLeod [very shaky signature]
Witnesses:
/s/ Murdoch Lamont
/s/ Donald Cameron, J.P. [wrote the will]
Proved 29 August 1873 by Murdoch Lamont."

From this we can deduce that Murdoch died between writing his will in November 1871 and the proving of it in August 1873.

George Sanborn says;

"The Murdoch McLeod estate is interesting as it names his two daughters Christy in the old Gaelic way. I got out my atlas, and the Murdoch McLeod property is the first one heading up the Junction Road from just below the church. Evidently the old house was on the larger portion of the 100 acres, lying to the right (north side of road) as one goes up the hill. I also got out the MacLeod book and there are almost two pages on this family. The book states that Murdoch was born about 1807 and came to P.E.I. in 1830 with his brothers Angus and Alexander (known as Sandy), leaving his wife, Euphemia MacDonald, and three children [Murdoch, Ann, and Christy the Elder] behind. The wife was known as Phebe (often a nickname for Euphemia).

About 1839 he sent for his wife and three children. Five more children were born in P.E.I. It looks as though he and his children must have been in Strathalbane in 1841, if the book is to be believed, and the five kids born in P.E.I. were all born there. The whole family consisted of: Murdoch; Ann; Christy the Elder; Margaret; John; Catherine (known as Kate); Christy the Younger; and Donald. [The book mistakenly assumes that the first Christy had died since they had a second child named Christy, but it was common in the Scottish Highlands for two siblings to share a Christian name!] The information was submitted by a George H. McLeod Jr. of Kernersville, North Carolina, a descendant of Donald. Indeed, the only one of Murdoch Sr.'s children about whom any information is presented is Donald. Donald married Johanna Buchanan of Hunter River. The book says that Donald was born 1839-1841, which suggests that he was first one born after the wife came out and joined Murdoch, but he is named last, so it's hard to tell how accurate the birth order in the list as presented really is.

We have an Alexander, who the Jubilee says came in 1830/31, in Lot 67. We have a wifeless Murdoch on the Lot 22 list who the Jubilee says came in 1831. We also have a slightly-older Angus in Lot 67, who the Jubilee says came in 1832/33. Are these our three brothers?"

These pieces of information confirm that Murdoch's farm was on the boundary of Lots 22 and 67, at Junction Road, and a look on 'Google Earth' clearly identifies the present-day property.

Brian Cox has now directed me to a Meacher's map of Lot 67; the property of Lady Wood, drawn by G. Wright, Surveyor in 1858 (all these names re-surfacing!). This plan shows two 100 acre farms, side by side, both in the names of Murdoch MacLeod, very likely father and son. Their neighbours are, as expected, Donald MacKinnon, James Nicholson, as well as the MacInnes, MacIntosh and Ross families with whom Murdoch sailed from Skye. (see appendix 3)

In 1871, the towns and villages of Prince Edward Island were enumerated and categorised. We have an entry for Springton. *"A village in the north parish of Queens. Distance from Charlottetown, a station of the New York, Newfoundland, and London Telegraph Co., 14, miles, from Princetown, 18 miles, from Georgetown 44 miles, from Summerside 20 miles. Mail bi-weekly. Population about 230."*

The document goes on to list all the family heads in the immediate area. Both Murdoch (probably Jr.) and Alexander MacLeod are noted as farmers and John MacLeod, carpenter. It is also interesting that Roderick and Donald MacIntosh and a widow MacIntosh are also shown (likely Ludvik MacIntosh's widow and two of their four sons).

In the equivalent 1880 Meacher map, Murdoch's sons, Murdoch (Jr) and John have the adjacent properties. John's share has the boundary between Lots 22 and 67 running through it! (see appendix 3)

The next farm but one to theirs, but on the Lot 67 side is the 100 acre property of Alexander MacLeod!

Further census information can be used to tell us more about Effy and family.

She appeared on the census in 1881 in Lot 67, Queens, Prince Edward Island.
Murdoch MCLEOD Male, Scottish, age 52, born Scotland, Farmer, Presbyterian. (i.e. Murdoch (Jr))
Effie MCLEOD Mother, Widow, Female, age 74, born Scotland, Presbyterian
John MCLEOD Brother, Male, age 32, born PE Island, Joiner, Presbyterian.
John M. VICKERSON Male, age 17, born PE Island, Joiner/ Student Presbyterian. (i.e. Ann's son)
Christy M. MCLEOD Female, age 30, born PE Island, Presbyterian
Margert(sic) N. NICHOLSON Female, age 15, born PE Island Presbyterian, (Perhaps one of Chirsty (the elder's children) or a household servant?)

She appeared on the census in 1891 in Lot 67 PEI.
McLeod Murdock M., 61, Head, Scotland, Presbyterian, Farmer
McLeod Effy Mrs. F., 83. Widow, Mother, Scotland, Presbyterian.

She appeared on the census in 1901 in Lot 67 PEI.
McLeod Donald M Head M 1841 60
McLeod Johana F Wife M Apr 9 1851 50
McLeod Bessie F Dauer S Aug 24 1882 18
McLeod Wesley M Son S Dec 6 1894 6
McLeod Murdoch M Bro S 1828 72
McLeod Effie F Mother W 1807 93
McLeod Dannie M Son S Sep 23 1887 13

By now our Effy, in spite of all of life's trials and tribulations had reached the advanced age of 93 but was to pass away later that year.

Obituary Notice in 'The Charlottetown Guardian' of August 16, 1901.

"Euphemia McDonald [MacDonald], aged 93, widow of the late Murdoch McLeod [MacLeod] ...... Mrs. McLeod and her husband were among the first settlers of that place [Lot 67] and experienced a full share of pioneer's hardships ...."

And from: The Morning Guardian, Charlottetown, P.E.I., Wed., 10 July 1901.

"On July 8th, 1901, at the advanced age of ninety-five years [sic], Euphemia McDonald, wife of the late Murdock McLeod, Springton,
Lot 67. Funeral from her late residence, on Wednesday, the 10th, to Springton Cemetery. The deceased was the mother of Mrs.
George Walker of this City [sic].

Our final interesting piece of research is her will;
Estates Division, P.E.I. Supreme Court
ESTATE OF EUPHEMIA McLEOD, SPRINGTON
Will. 1901. McL-848
Euphemia McLeod of Springton, Lot 67, widow of Murdoch McLeod of Springton, Lot 67
- "Depending now and for some time past on my son Donald for support, not only for myself but for my son Murdoch, I give all my real and personal estate to my son Donald. If my son Murdoch survives me, I hope Donald will look after him as heretofore. Donald is to have absolute power to sell my land, in whole or in part, and to satisfy himself for supporting me and my son Murdoch.

- After my death and my son Murdoch's death, if any residue remains, then up to $100.00 to be given to my grandson, John M. Vickerson within two years. Any funds that there might be over $100.00 are to be my son Donald's.
- My son Donald to be executor of my will."
3 December 1898 Euphemia [her X mark] McLeod
Witnesses:
/s/ Murdoch Lamont
/s/ Donald Lamont
Proved by Murdoch Lamont at Charlottetown 29 November 1901.
Inventory: Real estate, 100 acres of land at Springton, $2,000.00
Personal estate, $200.00
29 November 1901/s/ Murdoch Lamont.

We have further information on some of Murdoch and Effy's children and indeed, if more time were to be expended on research, I'm sure we could find out considerably more about their descendants.

The Old Portree Parish Records records the marriage of Murdo MacLeod and Effy MacDonald, both of Camustianavaig, on 6th January 1829 (see appendices) but does not register any of the children's births or baptisms but we had another surprise in store! On the 13th of February 1827 a 'natural' son, Kenneth Macleod was born to Effy MacDonald and Murdoch MacLeod. This birth **was** registered! Did Kenneth die young, since there is no more reference to him, or is he perhaps the Kenneth MacLeod, Sea Captain, born 1827, who appears aged 54 with his wife Jane and family in the 1881 Census for Charlottetown PEI! More research needed!

The marriage date suggests that at least one of the other children was illegitimate or that there were twins. Perhaps Effy's statement in Letter 1 "I was obliged to get married..." infers that there was considerable pressure on the couple to marry when she became pregnant for a second time!

Murdoch and Effy's family (see appendix 2)

Murdock Jr., Born 1828/29, Camustianavaig, Skye, Emigrated 1840, Farmer/Lay Preacher, Unmarried, Died after 1901.

'Murdoch McLeod (Murachadh Beag) was a man of rare intelligence, a good Gaelic and English scholar, equally conversant with both languages, but above all, he was a true and honest Christian, in every sense of the word. He was an orator of no mean order. He was really the first evangelist to Strathalbyn, and was for some years engaged in catechizing and preaching the word in the different settlements I referred to. When he would be on the rounds both old and young, would be in a flurry refreshing their memories on the questions of the shorter catechism. I believe he was instrumental in doing more real good in the place than perhaps any other man.' Historical Paper by Hon. A. B. MacKenzie 1895.

'He was a truly eloquent preacher of righteousness, and for hours held his audience spellbound...........It was under his faithful labours that the first revival of religion took place in the congregation, and to this day there are many who look back to him as their spiritual father.' 'History of Presbyterianism on Prince Edward Island' by John M. MacLeod 1904.

Ann, Born before 1831, Camustianavaig, Skye, Emigrated 1840, Married William Vickerson (b.1841-d. 1913) on 16th Oct. 1860 St James Presbyterian Church, Charlottetown, (two sons, George b.5 Nov 1861, d.13 Sept 1914 fostered by his Vickerson grandparents and John Murdoch b.17 Jul 1863 d. 1937 fostered by his MacLeod grandparents). Ann died 1863 (possibly in childbirth). (see appendix 6 for further information on John Murdoch Vickerson)

Christina (1), Born before 1831, Camustianavaig, Skye, Emigrated 1840, Married (husband unknown) with at least two children, Died before 1873.

Donald, Born 1841, Strathalbyn, Prince Edward Island, Married Johanna Buchanan (b. 1841 at Hunter River, PEI, d. 1946 at Spalding, Saskatewan) July 12, 1867 at Charlottetown, (at least 10 of a family), Died Jan. 19, 1914, when he fell through a roof. 1880 Atlas shows him holding 100 acres of land. (Census 1881, Lot 16 (Belmont), 1891, Lot 16, 1901, Lot 16 & Lot 67, 1911, Lot 17 (St Eleanor's)).

Margaret, Born abt 1844, Strathalbyn, Prince Edward Island.

Catherine (Kate), Born 1848, Strathalbyn, Prince Edward Island, Married Allan McLeod (1836-1915) on 6th Aug 1869 at Charlottetown, Died at Lot 16 after 1911.

Christina (II), Born 1851, Strathalbyn, Prince Edward Island, Married George Walker (1826-1907) at Charlottetown (see appendix 6 for information on her son).

John, Born abt 1849, Strathalbyn, Prince Edward Island.

Conclusion

So how successful have we been in answering the questions we set out in Chapter 2?

Who were they? Who were their relatives? Why did Murdo go? Why did Effy stay? Did Murdo come back for her and/or did Effy go alone? What became of their children? Was there a happy ending?

We now have answers to most of these questions but we cannot possibly know all of the personal circumstances. Our success in finding out about their grandchildren has been limited (see appendix 6) but perhaps some readers will be able to shed further light on the fate of Murdo and Effy's extended family.

How satisfying that this story which had such a traumatic beginning, has had a satisfying ending! But no, as fellow mortals, they did not live happily ever after, but some of them have inherited Glory!

An Imrich.	**The Emigration.**
"Siud an imrich tha feumail	"It is necessary to emigrate,
Dhol 'n ar leum as an fir s'	to hasten out of this land,
Do dh'America chraobhach,	and go to wooded America
'S am bi saors' agus sith.	where there will be freedom and peace.
Gheibh sinn fearann 'us aiteach	We shall get land and a home
Anns na fasaichean thall;	in the wilderness yonder;
Bidh na coilltean 'g an rusgadh	the forests will be cleared
Ged bhiodh cuinneadh oirnn gann.	though money will be scarce.

'N drasd 's ann tha sinn 'n ar
cruban
'M bothain udlaidh gun taing,
'Us na bailtean fo chaoraich
Aig luchd-maoine gun daimh.
Bidh am bradan air linne
'S cha bhi cion air na feidh;
Bidh gach eun air na crannaibh
Ann am barraibh nan geug;
Bidh an cruinneachd a' fas
dhuinn
'S bidh an t-al aig an spreidh.
Ma bhitheas againn ar slainte
Cha bhi cas orinn no eis.

'S mo ghuidhe ma sheolas sinn
Gu'n deonaichear dhuinn
Gu'm bi 'n Ti uile ghras-mhor
Dh' oidhch' 's a' la air ar stiuir,
Gu ar gleidheadh 's ar tear-
nadh
Bho gach gabhadh 'us cuis,
'S gu ar tabhairt Ian sabhailt
Do thir aghmhor na muirn."

Now we are cramped
in gloomy huts without
recompense,
and the fields are occupied
by sheep owned by the
unfriendly rich.
There will be salmon in the
lake,
and deer will not be wanting;
birds of every kind
will perch on the treetops;
wheat will grow for us,
and the herd will bear their
young.
If we but have health
we shall not be in want or
distress.

It is my wish, if we sail,
that it may be granted us
that the All Merciful One
guide us night and day,
to save us and protect us
from every peril and need,
and to bring us safely
to the land of good, cheer."

Composed by Rory Roy MacKenzie, passenger to Prince
Edward Island on the 'Polly'.

Appendices

Appendix 1

Copies of original fragments of Letter 1 which shows its condition and the difficulty in de-ciphering its contents.

Appendix 2

Murdoch and Effy's family

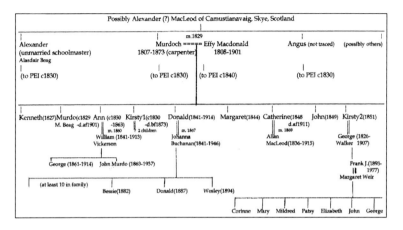

Appendix 3

Map 1 Camustianavaig Township 2010 (the crofts are the same size as in 1832)

The total area of the 12 crofts was 58acres. A single holding in PEI was 100acres! Total Common Pasture for the Camustianavaig Township was only 1024acres)

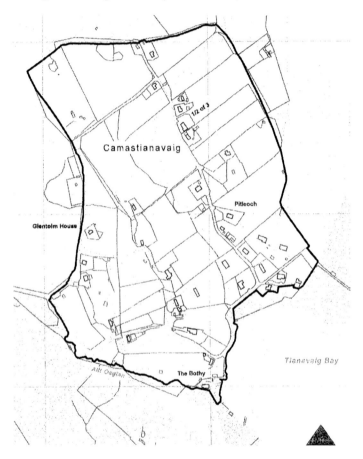

Map 2 Meacher's Map Lot 67 PEI 1858
(Note Murdoch (Jr) has 100acres on Lot 67, north of the border with Lot 22. His father has 100acres adjacent to him, but south of the line)

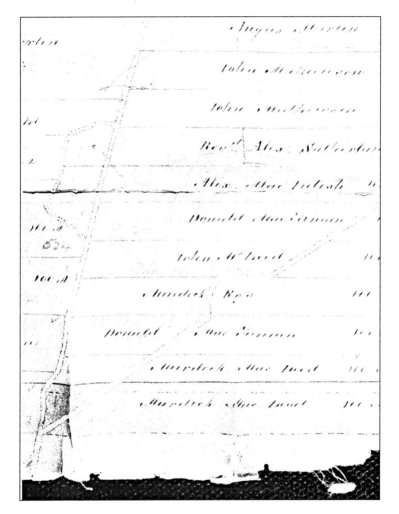

Map 3 Meacher's Map Lot 67 1880
(Note at the bottom of the map; Murdoch MacLeod Jr. on the
Lot 67 boundary and his brother John MacLeod across in Lot
22. Both properties are intersected by Junction Road.)

Map 4 Meacher's Map Lot 22 1878 showing their father's farm shared by the 2 brothers, as per the Murdoch (Sr) Will.
(also the names Alexander MacLeod, Neil MacLeod and Norman MacLeod re-surfacing)

Appendix 4

Old Portree Parish Record of the Marriage of Murdoch and Effy.

Appendix 5

Old Portree Parish Record of the birth of Kenneth MacLeod 'natural son' of Murdoch and Effy.
(transcript of extract as copy is difficult to decipher)

Kenneth nl. Son of   Murdoch Macleod   Portree 1827
&   Jan 13
EffyMacdonald

Appendix 6

Grandsons of Murdoch and Effy
Frank J. Walker

Frank J. Walker was born in Charlottetown, Prince Edward Island on 25 December 1893, the son of George and Christina (MacLeod) Walker. A few years after his father's death in 1907, he dropped out of high school and apprenticed as a machinist with Bruce Stewart & Company. Four days after the declaration of World War I, he enlisted as a private and served in the Canadian Field Ambulance, Army Medical Corps, First Canadian Contingent as a stretcher bearer, seeing active service in France at some of the major battles of the Western Front before being invalided out after the battle of Passchendaele. Following his recovery in hospitals and casualty depots in England he served on the hospital ships "Neuralia" and "Essequibo" running between England and Canada. During the war he kept a diary and wrote poetry, also contributing to the Medical Corps newssheet "The Iodine Chronicle". In 1918, he also published a small booklet of poems entitled "Flanders from a stretcher handle".

After demobilization, he returned briefly to Bruce Stewart and Co. but in the early 1920's became a reporter for the Guardian newpaper under the editorship of James Robertson Burnett. His first reporting assignment was in the press gallery of the provincial legislature and he became known as "Mr. Hansard" for his painstakingly accurate reporting of the proceedings at a time when there was no official Hansard. He later became editor of the Guardian and his views and editorials helped to shape the public opinion of his day. He was a strong supporter of Prince Edward Island's rights within Confederation. He was also fascinated by Island history and between 1946 and 1955 presented a weekly column for the paper entitled "Old Charlottetown".

(In October 1946 a small one column article appeared in the "Charlottetown Guardian" under the heading of "Old

Charlottetown". From then until 1955 Islanders were treated to an eclectic selection of items relating to the early history of the city and the Island. Although others such as Major T.E. MacNutt also contributed to the column it was Frank Walker who provided the majority of the selections and presented them to the public. The items were drawn from a wide range of published sources but primarily from newspapers in the Legislative Library collection. The published sources were often rare volumes containing incidents long-forgotten by the majority of Islanders. Selections covered the major events such as Confederation as well as social history. The more off-beat an item was the more likely it was to appear in "Old Charlottetown".)

After 35 years as a reporter and editor, Frank Walker, suffering from ill health retired from the Guardian in 1969. He was married to Margaret Weir with whom he had five daughters and two sons: Corinne, Mary, Mildred, Patsy, Elizabeth, John and George. Frank Walker died in Charlottetown on 24 November 1977.

Following Frank Walker's death, the volumes containing the clippings went missing but were eventually located by Bill Burnett, a fellow newspaperman, who recognized their research value and passed them on to the Public Archives and Records Office in April of 1990.

Series 1: A war journal, by Frank Walker [World War I, 8 August, 1914- 22 July 1917 + postscript
Series 2: Scrapbooks of "Old Charlottetown (and PEI)"; articles from the "Guardian" newspaper.

John Murdoch Vickerson (born 1863 died 1937 in California)

John Murdock Vickerson is one of the highly respected citizens of Burlingame, San Mateo County, California, USA who, after a long, active and successful business career, is now retired from active affairs and is enjoying well earned leisure. Born in Canada, he is a son of William and Ann (McLeod) Vickerson, both of whom were natives of that country, where the father engaged in farming and stock raising. John M. Vickerson attended the public schools of his home neighborhood and in 1892 came to California. For the past thirty years he has resided in San Mateo county and for many years engaged in building and contracting, in which he built up a large business, gaining an enviable reputation as a reliable and competent contractor, many of the best buildings in this section of the state standing in evidence of his careful and painstaking work. He carried on this business until about five years ago, when he retired. In 1897 Mr. Vickerson was united in marriage to Miss Elizabeth McInnis, who also is a native of Canada and is a daughter of Kenneth and Mary Ann (McLeod) McInnis. She attended the public schools of the Dominion and completed her education in Prince of Wales College. She is a past president of the Burlingame Women's Club, a past president of the North Burlingame Community Club, a member of the Presidents' Assembly of San Francisco and for the past ten years has served as a member of the school board. She is also a communicant of the Protestant Episcopal church of Burlingame. Mr. and Mrs. Vickerson have been worthy citizens of this community, taking a commendable interest in its progress and welfare, and hold a high place in, the esteem and confidence of all who know them. (Written about 1930)

Information from Anna-Lee Hogan of Charlottetown PEI.

Appendix 7

An 1846 summary of the 'New' Statistical Account of 1841 written by the Parish Minister Rev. Coll Macdonald.

EMIGRATION FROM THE ISLE OF SKYE.

TOWN AND HARBOUR OF PORTREE.

PORTREE, a parish, mostly in the Isle of Skye, and wholly in the county of Inverness; including the islands of Fladda, Rasay, and Rona; and containing 3574 inhabitants, of whom 510 are in the village of Portree, 25 miles (N. W.) from Broadford, 21 (E.) from Dunvegan, 80 (N. by E.) from Tobermory, 110 (N. by W.) from Obau, and 109 (W. by S.) from Inverness. This place was formerly called *Ceilltarraglan*, a compound Gaelic term which signifies "a burying-ground at the bottom of a glen," and which was particularly appropriate; but after the visit of King James V. to the northern portion of his dominions, and his putting into the bay here, where he remained for some time, the name was changed to Portree, or *Port-roi* or *righ*, "the King's harbour." The parish consists of the portion properly called Portree, and the islands of Rasay, Rona, and others of small extent, separated from the main body by a branch of the

Atlantic Ocean, called Rasay sound. It measures seventeen miles in length and twelve in breadth, and is principally a pastoral district, the quantity of land under tillage being but very small in comparison with the part uncultivated. On the east is an arm of the sea dividing Rasay from the parishes of Gairloch and Applecross. The long line of coast exhibits great diversity of appearance: its lofty and almost perpendicular rocks are succeeded in some places, especially at the heads of the lochs, by sudden depressions sinking almost to the level of the beach; and the shores are intersected by numerous breaks and fissures. Among the bays are those of Loch Inord, Loch Sligichan, Camistinavaig, and several small bays in the island of Rasay; but that of Portree is by far the most considerable, and is capable of containing several hundred sail, shelter on all sides being afforded by very high lands, and its tenacious clayey bottom supplying excellent anchorage. The Rasay branch of the Atlantic, which washes the parish throughout its whole length, is sufficiently deep for the passage of a first-rate ship of war. It receives a large influx of fresh water from the hills on each side, bringing down earthy deposits which, from the rapidity of the currents in its friths, render it turbid and dark in wintry or stormy weather; but in the tranquillity of summer it is beautifully clear.

The surface in the interior is varied with hills, valleys, and plains, interspersed with innumerable springs of the purest water, several lakes and rivulets, and some highly ornamented cascades, which together render the scenery deeply interesting. The district is circumscribed by a most circuitous and irregular outline, approaching in its general form to an oblong, and is traversed from south to north by a glen, skirted on each side by a range of hills greatly differing in height and dimensions. The most striking elevation is that called *Aite Suidhe Fhin*, "the sitting-place of Fingal," where that celebrated hero is traditionally reported to have sat to direct his followers in the chase, and which, rising gradually from the head of Loch Portree, reaches 2000 feet above the level of the sea. Near this, on the east side of the harbour, and of almost equal height with the former, rises the hill of Peindinavaig, or "the hill of protection;" while much to the south are the hill of Beinligh, and that of Glamaig, with the loch of Sligichan between them. The latter is crowned with a verdant tract, and has a spring sending forth an immense quantity of clear water: indeed all the elevations, with slight exceptions, are covered to their summits with excellent pasture for sheep and cattle, and are well watered with springs and rivulets. There are six fresh-water lochs, most of which abound in good trout; and though of no great extent, the largest not being above a mile long, they exhibit much picturesque and beautiful scenery, enriched, in Rasay, with clumps of natural wood, or grotesque rocks. From their vicinity may be seen the celebrated hills of Cullins, in the parish of Bracadale, and of Store, in the parish of Snizort; and from a loch in Rasay, in favourable weather, a very fine prospect may be had of all the hills in the district, to the point of Hunish. with the expanse of sea to the island of Lewis. The climate is one of the most variable to be found, many descriptions of weather being frequently experienced within the space of a day and night; and diseases arising from the sudden changes of temperature, are often prevalent.

The soil between the hills is to a great extent peatmoss, whence the inhabitants are amply supplied with their ordinary fuel; but that most general is a gravelly earth, abounding in springs. These render the land raw and unproductive; and in addition to the natural sterility of the soil, the poverty of the inhabitants, and their necessarily imperfect system of husbandry, the vicissitude of the weather, either in seed-time or in harvest, and sometimes in both, often destroys at once the hopes of the year. The whole of the main land part of the parish belongs to Lord Macdonald; and the island of Rasay, with its subordinate isles, to Macleod, of Rasay. The former proprietor, about the year 1811, for the accommodation of the rapidly increasing population, caused all the farms held by small tenants to be subdivided into allotments or crofts. This has tended still further to increase the number of persons here located; and the inhabitants now so far exceed the productive capabilities of the soil, as to place the tenants upon the lowest possible scale with respect to the comforts of life, as well as to keep the land far below the average state of that in neighbouring districts. The crooked spade is used, and is well suited to the peculiar character of the surface, the arable portion frequently hanging on steeps and precipices, and being set with rocks or large stones; and after the seed is sown the hollows and inequalities are neatly raked over, and smoothed with a hand-harrow. Even were the tenants competent to the undertaking, the land is incapable of successful draining, as its fixed watery nature, arising from springs, would soon cause it to revert to its original spongy character. The crofters live in huts of the meanest condition, and are often without proper food and clothing; this however is in no way attributable to any want of disposition to promote improvements, but to poverty and destitution which they are unable to controul. Their sobriety and general character are spoken of in the highest terms; and this circumstance has induced the proprietor, for these few last years, to expend considerable sums of money in sending part of the population to the British colonies in North America.

A large tract in the parish is undivided common, consisting of hill pasture which is covered in the summer months with cattle, which are small but hardy, and mostly out of shelter for the whole year. They are supported in the winter on straw; but after feeding at the return of spring on the pasture, which is chiefly mossgrass, they acquire strength and flesh, and are carried off by the south-country dealers in large numbers, to fatten for the markets of England, where they are much esteemed, and fetch a high price. The sheep are a cross between the native stock and the black-faced of the south; the horses, though very small, are hardy. The breeds of cattle and sheep are much attended to; and great improvements have recently taken place in consequence of the stimulus given by the premiums of the Highland and local agricultural societies, and especially by the facilities of conveyance to the leading markets by steam navigation. Coal was wrought about the beginning of the present century by Lord Macdonald; but the expense, after a regular system of operations had been for some time carried on by experienced colliers from the south, proved so great that the quantity raised was not sufficient to remunerate the proprietor, and the work was abandoned. Excellent granite is found in several places, particularly in Rasay, and, being of very hard texture, is formed into millstones for grinding oats and barley, which are sold at from £9 to £12 per pair, and supply all the mills in Skye and the neighbouring parishes. Limestone is abundant; and at Portree, on both sides of the harbour, freestone is found in very large quantities in the lofty rocks, which are nearly perpendicular. Stone of the same species, but of far superior quality, is obtained in great plenty in Rasay; and some of it was used in building, a few years since, the elegant mansion of the proprietor of the island, the only gentleman's seat in the parish. Near this residence are some fine old trees; but the other wood in the parish is only plantation of Scotch fir, larch, birch, ash, and oak, of recent formation, and situated principally in the island of Rasay and the village of Portree.

The village, in which the population amounts to above 500, is ornamented by some pretty plantations, and contains several good houses and shops, and a branch establishment of the National Bank of Scotland. The sheriff-substitute of the district of Skye holds his courts in the court-room of the gaol here, as the superintendent of the judicial affairs of the place; and there is a post-office having a regular delivery of letters three times a week. A road has been formed through the whole length of the parish, under the direction of the parliamentary commissioners for building bridges and making roads in the Highlands and islands; and Glasgow steam-boats, weekly in the summer, and monthly in the winter, come into the harbour, by which means the cattle and other produce are sent to the southern markets. Salmon, also, the fishing of which belongs to a small company from the south, is cured in the village, and forwarded by the same conveyance to Glasgow and London. Three fairs are held, respectively in May, July, and November, the two former for the sale of black-cattle, and the latter for the hiring of servants and for other business. The rateable annual value of the parish is £3195. It is in the presbytery of Skye and synod of Glenelg, and in the patronage of the Crown: the minister's stipend is £150, of which about one-half is received from the exchequer; with a manse, and a glebe, consisting principally of moss and hill pasture, and valued at £11 per annum. The church, built about the year 1820, for the accommodation of 800 persons with sittings, is situated in the village, but on account of its distance from the southern boundary, which is fifteen miles off, is inconvenient for a considerable portion of the population. A missionary is stationed in the parish, on the establishment of the committee of the General Assembly, and receives a salary from the bounty allowed by the crown for the benefit of the Highlands. The parochial school, also situated in the village, affords instruction in Latin, Greek, geography, book-keeping, and English, in addition to the elementary branches; the master has a salary of £34. 4., with a house, an allowance for a garden, and £5 fees. There is a branch parochial school in Rasay, in which the elementary branches only are taught; also two schools where the instruction is in Gaelic, this being the vernacular tongue.

Source: Portree Local History Society Website.

Appendix 8

Hardships and Coffin Ships!

"An t-earrach seo agus seo chaidh	"This Spring and last Spring
's gach fichead earrach bho 'n an tùs	and every twenty Springs from the beginning,
tharruing ise 'n fheamainn fhuar	she has carried the cold
chum biadh a cloinne 's duais an tùir."	seaweed for her children's food and the castle's reward."

Sorley MacLean

There were lots of positive factors which made emigration from Skye to Prince Edward Island attractive, and a number of negative factors co-incided during the 19th century, to make the lot of the people of Braes increasingly difficult at home. Some of these have been previously mentioned but, as time went by, many of them were exacerbated.

As a result of the turbulence following the failed rebellion of 1745, the Snizort area of Skye suffered particularly badly. Snizort, unlike the rest of Trotternish, which was MacDonald territory, was in the possession of the Raasay MacLeods, who had joined Bonny Prince Charlie's cause. The chiefs of MacDonald and MacLeod of Harris had vacillated and indulged in fence sitting, so, to a certain extent, their people escaped retribution. Many of the Snizort people emigrated, but others who remained in Skye, moved to neighbouring parishes. The Braes district received several families from that area. Likewise, when Lord MacDonald's deer forest was created in central Skye, numbers of people from the Sconser area were uprooted and settled in Braes. The crofters of *Coillemhor*, a Sconser township, had been deprived of their hill grazing and were forbidden to keep sheep and so felt pressured to move. Later, in 1853, when Ballingall, the chief's Factor, decided to enlarge the deer forest, *"two families of crofters and seven cottars were cleared off Aricharnach, eight from Moll and sixteen crofters, in addition to several squatters, were removed from Ceann nan Creagan and Tormicheag"*. (Evidence to the Napier Commission)

The already overcrowded crofts in the Braes townships had now to be sub-divided and houses built for the additional population. Most of the tiny crofts now had three and some-times four families living on them.

Secondly, the kelp industry, which had at least provided work and a small wage for many families, began to decline. After the Napoleonic Wars, the ban on importation of barilla from Spain was lifted, the salt tax was removed and large potash deposits were discovered in Germany. These factors drove down the price payable for kelp ash, so that its produc-tion became totally uneconomic. In 1841, the Rev A. Clark, a Skye minister, commented that the 80 tons of kelp produced in his parish that year did; *"little more than repay the cost of making it"*.

Another commentator said; *"When the manufacture of kelp was brisk, there was no crofter who, after paying rent, had not an abundant supply of meal for his family but now they are in a wretched condition."*

About this time the MacDonald Estate Factor began explor-ing the possibility of extracting coal from a narrow seam which runs from Ollach in Braes to Camus Ban in Portree Bay. Some historians have interpreted this as a laudable effort on the part of the Estate to procure paying work for the redundant kelp workers. I think not, as he also brought miners from the south of Scotland to undertake the work! As it happened, the coal mine was not a success, as the seam only consisted of low calo-rific value lignite (brown coal).

A third and very significant factor in impoverishing the people was the continued importation of sheep and shepherds from the Scottish Borders.

Sheep farming came to Skye at the start of the 19th century, and it has been claimed that it was first introduced by the

MacAskills of Minginish. The new breeds were branded with an 'S' and known in the district as 'Rhundunan' sheep. As early as 1803 a Kenneth MacAskill was complaining to fellow farmers about the cost and delays in getting customs clearance for shipment of wool to Liverpool. A few years later an agricultural survey reported, "Sheep have lately been introduced as farm stock at Rhundunan, Gesto and Tallisker and they promise to do well. They are indeed the only proper stock for the Cuillin mountain districts."

The MacDonald Estate, like others, began to see the potential for sheepstock as the price of wool rose. Not only were the local people deprived of their traditional grazings to make way for the voracious 'caoraich mhor', there was no decrease in their croft rental and there was no employment for them in the sheep industry.

"When the bold kindred, in the time long-vanished,
Conquered the soil and fortified the keep—
No seer foretold the children would be banished,
That a degenerate lord might boast his sheep:

Fair these broad meads, these hoary woods are grand;
But we are exiles from our fathers' land."
(Canadian Boat Song. Anon.)

When there was a further downturn in the herring fishing trade and the potato crop failed, the people of Braes faced disaster and dire poverty.

By 1846 and 1847 the Government was urgently requested to send fast naval steam ships to Portree with emergency supplies of meal to help feed a starving population.

"It is however perfectly evident that no liberality on the part of the proprietors can render the present immense surplus population in any measure comfortable. And there is, humanly speaking, no other way to provide for them than emigration; though certainly,

it would be for ever a matter of regret, that so noble a race of men should be under the necessity of leaving their native land and seeking an asylum on a foreign shore. But, as they are unable to effect this by any means within their own reach, they should be conveyed to any British settlement which may be thought eligible – all the expense defrayed, and lands provided for them in their adopted settlement, by the Government of the country."
Rev Coll MacDonald, Portree. 1841

Emigrant ships

It is important to remember that not all of the voyages from Scotland to Canada were as trouble free as the ones we have been so far concerned with. John MacLeod in his book on the Highland Clearances, *'No Great Mischief if you Fall'* tells us that *"Between 1847 and 1853, at least forty-nine ships laden with forced Highland emigrants were lost at sea."*

But Lucille Campey insists in *"A Very Fine Class of Immigrants"*: *"Between 1847 and 1851, forty British ships were wrecked at sea with a loss of 1,043 lives, but almost all the people who died were Irish. Never before or since have so many fatalities or so much suffering been endured at sea. But although this was especially an Irish horror story, its impact has been allowed to envelop the whole history of emigrant sea travel. By burying the comparatively miniscule Scottish immigrant numbers in with the Irish figures, some later commentators have given the deeply erroneous impression that high death rates occurred on Scottish crossings – when they did not".*

There are numerous other documents which tell us that not everything to do with emigration was sweetness and light! There seems to be a tendancy on the Canadian side of the Atlantic to paint a very positive picture of both the voyages and the condition of the people who arrived in Prince Edward Island. Often we are assured by their descendants that *"these were not paupers"*, *"a very fine class of immigrants"*, and that they were relatively prosperous and well prepared for the vigours of a pioneering life; while on the Skye side the version is of an impoverished people desperate to get away, having sold all their possessions for a pittance. Doubtless the truth lies somewhere between the two extremes.

"During the last week of July 1840 a full rigged ship and a brig left Loch Snizort for Prince Edward Island. The ship contained 400 people and the brig 200. The brig crossed in 31 days while the ship, due to poor navigation and losing its way, took 8 weeks. During the journey 9 passengers died on board and four or five babies were born."

It is very likely that the latter part of this statement applies to the expected ship whose arrival I was unable to trace.

(see Chapter 11

The '*Royal Gazette*' of 24th August went on to say about the Skye folk; *"They are a hardy vigorous set of people – not a pauper among them. Two other vessels from Tobermory are looked for Daily."* One of these was the '*Heroine*' of Aberdeen with 281 passengers. She sailed via Stornoway, arriving in Charlotetown 37 days later. I have failed to trace any information on the other.)

Most trips certainly went well but there were occasions when fever broke out on the more crowded ships or the weather was unfavourable or the ships were trapped in ice or fog-bound. Sometimes conditions must have been horrendous! As Walter Riddell, passenger on the '*Lancaster*' recounts:

"Last night about 10 o'clock we got among a field of ice; it was that thick we could see no way through it; about 6 a m the Captain appeared to be drunk and the seamen would not obey his orders; at the same time one of the seamen got his thigh bone broken between the yard and the mast; the Captain having hold of the helm, ran the ship betwixt two pieces of ice and some of the seamen cried we are all gone! One ran and took the Captain from the helm; they struggled together until some of the men inter-posed; the Captain threatened dreadfully what he would do when we reached Quebec; saw a vessel to the windward of us; about 10

am the ice cleared away and we saw no more of it. We were scarcely out of the ice when the wind blew about a hurricane from the south-east … the waves were bigger than I have ever seen them".

Another Walter, Walter Johnstone, passenger on the *'Diana'*, says:

"All the passengers, forty-five in number, later became more or less seasick. On the 28th day we saw American land, supposedly the south side of Cape Breton, but the fog was so thick we could only discern the shore, and had to stand out to sea and steer back-wards and forwards on the banks of Newfoundland for eight days. When it cleared, passing Cape North, we entered the Gulf of St. Lawrence. On Friday morning we made Prince Edward Island about nine o'clock, rising like a dark cloud from the bosom of the ocean".

At the Museum of the Isles at Armadale there is a very thought provoking notice:-

"Imagine you are lying in a space not much bigger than a large double bed. You are not on your own. You share this space, a glorified bunk, with your whole family. Either side of you, stretch-ing away into the distance, there are other bunks. There are more above you, just a few feet away. At the foot of your bunk, across a passageway, there is another double row of bunks. It is dark and stuffy. The air smells. There are too many people crammed into a small dark space. You are on an emigrant ship, sailing away to a new life in Australia or North America."

As a child, a certain Donald Martin of Monkstadt was deeply saddened as he heard the wailing of the passengers on board an emigrant ship at Uig. They were leaving their kith and kin forever and voyaging out into the unknown. It is difficult for us in the 21st century to appreciate the trauma that these occasions must have provoked, both for those who left and for those who stayed. *'I watched that ship as she sailed away, and ever since and now, I have asked myself and others, the reason why'*.

Many have formed the conclusion that 'the main reason why' was man's inhumanity to man!

In complete contrast to the sadness of leaving Skye; how delighted these emigrants must have been to make land-fall in their new home. But excitement and anticipation soon waned in the case of some. A Canadian, Dundas Warder wrote of some immigrants: *"We have been pained beyond measure for some time past to witness in our streets so many unfortunate Highland emigrants, apparently destitute of all means of subsistence, and many of them sick from want and other attendant causes. It was pitiful the other day to view a funeral of one of these wretched people. It was, indeed, a sad procession. The coffin was constructed of the rudest material; a few rough boards nailed together was all that could be afforded to convey to its last resting-place the body of a homeless emigrant. Children followed in the mournful train; perchance they followed a brother's bier, one with whom they had sported and played for many a healthful day among their native glens. Theirs were looks of indescribable sorrow. They were in rags; their mourning weeds were the shapeless fragments of what had once been clothes. There was a mother, too, among the mourners, one who had tended the departed with anxious care in infancy, and had doubtless looked forward to a happier future in this land of plenty. The anguish of her countenance told too plainly these hopes were blasted and she was about to bury them in the grave of her child."*

As far as we can gather, none of the Skye emigrants to Prince Edward Island arrived in such conditions. Perhaps they were fortunate in the agents who made arrangements for their reception and ship's captains who had taken care to convey them in safety and a degree of cleanliness.

Appendix 9

Who were they?

"Cha b'i crionach liath no mosgan,

Bho'n a shiolaich treud an fhortainn;

Ach fiodh miath, gun mhiar, gun socadh,

Geal mar ghrian, bho bhian Rìgh Lochluinn."

Donald MacLeod *(Do'ull nan Oran)*

"It was not from hoary or dead wood

That the fortunate tribe derived

But from healthy timber without knot or water-logging,

A kindred white like the Sun from the lustre of the King of Norway."

(Donald of the Songs)

Scottish Highlanders have a fundamental sense of place and belonging, and so there are two important Gaelic questions that are always asked of an individual; *Cò as a tha thu?* and *Cò leis thu?* (Where do you come from? and To whom do you belong?)

Murdoch and Effy were descended from different clans. Murdoch was a MacLeod and Effy a MacDonald. History tells us that for hundreds of years, and well into the 18th Century, MacLeods and MacDonalds were sworn enemies. So how had their families become neighbours in the township of Camustianavaig?

First of all we must look back at the histories of Skye's clans.

The Gaelic word *clan* means 'the children'. So the members of Clan MacLeod are the children of *Leod*.

In his authoritative and very readable *'History of Skye'*, Alexander Nicolson succeeds in de-mistifying the origins of our clans.

The MacLeods

Leod was believed to be the son of *Olaf the Black*, King of Man, a Norseman who had married Christina, daughter of Farquhar, Earl of Ross.

Màiri ni'n Alasdair Ruaidh, one of Clan MacLeod's famous bards, seems to confirm this Norse origin when she speaks of a MacLeod warrior as:

> *"Fuil dhìreach Righ Lochluinn*
> *B'e sud toiseach do sheanachais."*
> "The direct blood of the Norse king
> That was the beginning of your lineage."

The Norsemen, or Vikings, had controlled the islands of the north and west of Scotland for some 400 years until the defeat of Norway's *King Haakon* at the hands of *Alexander III* of Scotland, at the Battle of Largs in 1263. This led, three years later, to the Treaty of Perth in which Haakon's successor, *King Magnus,* gave up all claims to the Scottish Islands. This, however, was far from the end of Norse influence on the islands and it is well attested that many of the clans had a Norse origin.

The poet goes further and says of the MacLeod warrior:

> *"Lochlannaich threun, toiseach do sgeuil,*
> *Sliochd solta bho fhreumh Mhànuis."*
> "Strong Norseman you derive your line,
> Lush seed from the stock of Magnus."

Leod was born at the beginning of the 13th Century and fostered, in his early youth, to *Paul Balkeson*, the powerful Lord and Sheriff of Skye. In 1231, when *Balkeson* died, *Leod* fell heir to parts of Skye, Uist and Harris, which he added to his many other possessions namely; the Isle of Lewis from his father, the lands of Glenelg, from his maternal grandfather, the *Earl of Ross*, and many other parts of north and west Skye by his judicious marriage to the daughter of another Norse chieftain, *MacRaild* or *(Mac-Harold)*. (Some historians believe that the name Lewis *(Leodhas)*, derives from the Norse name *Leod Huis* [the home of Leod]).

MacRaild's former castle of Dunvegan became the head-quarters of one of Leod's two sons, *(Tormod)*, *Norman* (styled MacLeod of Harris), while the Isle of Lewis remained the home of *(Torquil)* (styled MacLeod of Lewis). The successors of these two sons became the progenitors of two distinct clans. *Siol Thormoid* and *Siol Thorcuil*.

If we digress for a little and consider another clan of Norse origin, we will understand how the *Siol Thorcuil* came to claim the Island of Raasay on Skye's east coast.

Like Skye, there is evidence that Raasay was occupied in Stone-age times by itinerant peoples, but the earliest known perma-nent residents were Vikings known as the *MacSweens* (Children of *Sven*), their descendants in Canada use the spelling *MacSwain*. It is believed that they built and fortified Brochel Castle. The last *MacSween* Chief of Raasay, *Iain Mor*, was renowned for valour, but had no heir. As was the habit in those early days, the *MacSween* Chief, around 1520, adopted *Malcolm*, second son of *Torquil MacLeod* of Lewis, who came to live at Brochel Castle. Following some dispute, *Malcolm (Calum)* murdered his foster father at *Tobar a' Chinn* at *Drumuie* near Portree and claimed the Island of Raasay for himself. His clan became known as *Clan Mac Ghille Chaluim* and they ruled Raasay until 1846 when the 13th MacLeod Chief, *Mac Ghille Chaluim XIII* sold the island to a *Mr. George Rainy*.

As well as the lands of Raasay, the *Mac Ghille Challuim* Chiefs held, for many years, some lands in Snizort parish Skye, including Eyre, Tote, Carbost, Glengrasgo, Uigishader and Rigg. These tacks were farmed by cadets of the clan.

Because *Malcolm*, the 10th Chief had joined the Jacobite Cause in the 1745 Rebellion, his people and lands on Raasay and Snizort suffered terribly in the aftermath of Culloden.

Alexander Nicolson, quoting a report of that time, tells us that *"the lands of the Raasay MacLeods on Skye did not escape. So terrible, indeed, was the devastation wrought there, that families were forced to evacuate their homes, fleeing to neighbouring districts and leaving waste their own lands, ("as they are to this day" —- quote 1748)"*

A cousin of Chief *Malcolm* was *Norman MacLeod*, tacksman of Rigg, who had married *Jane MacQueen*, daughter of the tacksman of Totarome. As a result of anti-Jacobite punishment most of their family moved, as feudal inferiors, to the Braes area, south of Portree, to farm land belonging to the *MacDonalds of Sleat*.

Two of *Norman* and *Jane's* sons became eminent soldiers in the British Army during the American War of Independence – Captain *Norman of Camustianavaig* and Lieutenant *John of Ollach*. John's heirs still held the Upper Ollach tack from 1823 to 1829.

Collation of evidence from several sources suggests that our **Murdoch MacLeod** was possibly a grandson or grandnephew of Captain *Norman MacLeod of Camustianavaig*.

The MacDonalds

Clan MacDonald, like several other Scottish clans, has its origin in the semi-mythical and Celto-Norse, *Gillabrigte*. Macdonald tradition tells us that this warrior had lands in the isles which were raided by the Norsemen. He took refuge in a cave in Morven and became known as *Gillabrigte na h-Uamha*, *Gillabrigte* of the cave.

The Vikings had taken control of the *Nordreys* (northern isles, Orkneys and Shetlands) and *Sudreys* (southern isles, Isle of Man and isles of Scotland's west coast), about 1100 AD under the command of *Magnus Barelegs* and his sons *Lagman* and *Olaf Bitling*. Much intermarriage between Celt and Viking took place, and the people of the *Sudreys* became known as the

Gall-Gaedhil or foreign Gaels. In Gaelic tradition, *Olaf Bitling* was known as *Olaf the Red* and it was in the days of his power that *Somerled*, a son of *Gillabrigte na h-Uamha* came to prominence. The name *Somerled* means Summer-voyager or Viking, which suggests that, although his father was a Gael, his mother was Norse. By the year 1140 *Somerled* was a very powerful man on Scotland's west coast, having sent men to fight on the side of Scotland's King *David I*, against England, at the Battle of the Standard in 1138. So powerful in fact that he was seen as a threat to the kingdom of *Olaf the Red, King of Man and the Isles*. Having made a political marriage to *Ranghild, Olaf's* daughter, *Somerled* positioned himself for control of the Scottish Isles. When *Olaf* was murdered by his nephews, *Somerled* named his eldest son *Dougall (Olaf's* grandson), *King of the Isles*. By 1158 *Somerled* and his three sons had forced the Norsemen out of nearly all their west coast possessions and, with the blessing of King *Malcolm IV*, laid the foundations for centuries of Gaelic sea-power. By 1164, however, *Somerled* had revolted against the King of Scotland and was to die at the Battle of Renfrew and be buried in Iona.

Somerled's three sons, *Dougall, Ranald* and *Angus* divided Argyle and the Islands between them, but internecine rivalry spelled the end of *Angus's* family. This is the time when history begins to record patronymics and the *MacDougall* clan derived from *Somerled's* eldest son. Likewise the *MacDonalds* and the *MacRuaris* were derived from *Ranald's* two sons *Donald* and *Ruari*.

Donald became established first in the Island of Islay and his son *Angus Mor* was the first of millions of MacDonalds in History!

By 1336 the progeny of *Donald of Islay* had taken the title *Lords of the Isles*, a title which has now been reclaimed by royalty and currently rests with *Prince Charles, Prince of Wales*. When in Scotland he is known as *Duke of Rothesay* and *Lord of the Isles*.

By 1440 the *Lords of the Isles* had reached their peak of political power in Scotland under the *3rd Lord, Alexander,* who died in 1449. His eldest son *John* succeeded to the title while his other two sons – *Celestine* received the lands of Lochalsh, Lochcarron and Lochbroom – and *Hugh* began the great family of the MacDonalds of Sleat, *Clann Uisdein,* who were destined to take over as the *High Chiefs* when future illegitimate grandsons of *John* were barred from the title. In 1493 the dignity of the *Lordship of the Isles* was extinguished and clan chiefs were required to seek royal charters for lands which they occupied.

In 1539, *Donald Gorm*, the 6th Chief of *Clann Uisdein*, with the help of the *MacLeod's of Lewis*, finally expelled the *MacLeods of Harris (and Dunvegan)* from *Trotternish* and the MacDonalds' main seat became *Duntulm Castle,* until this estate was confiscated after the 1715 Rebellion.

So where do the MacDonalds of Braes come from?

The late, knowledgeable, John MacDonald (*Shonnie Ivie*), who so ably assisted the archivist at the Clan Donald Centre at Armadale in Skye, was of the opinion that the MacDonald families of *Conordon* and *Camustianavaig* in the *Braes of Trotternish* were descended from the MacDonalds of *Cnocowe* near *Duntulm*. Other historians maintain that their progenitor may have been *Hugh MacDonald of Glenmore*, father of Rev. Hugh MacDonald, Portree's first parish minister, who died in 1756 aged 57.

I believe that *Shonnie Ivie's* view was shared by the late poet and genealogist Dr. Sorley MacLean who told me that the first of the Braes' MacDonalds lived at *Scorr* on the steep slopes to the south of Portree Bay.

Either way, *Hugh MacDonald of Glenmore* and *John MacDonald of Balgown and Cnocowe* were half-brothers, sons of *Sir James Mor*, 10th Chief and 2nd Baronet of Sleat.

In 1661, Sir James married Mary MacLeod, sister of *Iain Breac MacLeod of Dunvegan* as his second wife. Their son *John*, with the consent of *Donald*, his half-brother and *Sir James'* heir, was given the wadset (lease) of *Monkstadt and Cnocowe*. In about 1720, with his estates under sentence of forfeiture, and the rents being collected and paid to Government Commissioners, the then 13th Chief and 5th Baronet, *Sir Donald*, was forced to abandon *Duntulm Castle* and was kindly given occupancy of *Monkstadt House* by *John* who moved his own home across the hill to *Cnocowe*. There is a tradition that the abandonment of the Castle was actually as a result of the chief's infant son falling to his death on the rocks below the castle window.

John's successors at *Cnocowe* were in turn, *Aonghas Ruadh*, *Donald Ruadh* and *Raonull Ruadh*. This *Raonull* or Ronald was said to have had a family of 21, most of whom emigrated to Prince Edward Island and Cape Breton in the very early 1800s.

Could it be that our **Effy** already had many cousins on 'The Island'?

William MacKenzie in his *"Old Skye Tales"* says *"Almost all the Cnocowe MacDonalds whom I have been able to trace, have a Hugh in the family"*. But Hugh was, of course, a very common name among the families of the MacDonalds of Sleat, as they were *Clann Uisdein,* (children of Hugh).

Effy's father was a Hugh MacDonald, born in 1766!

Was he perhaps an elder brother of my own great-great-great-grandfather, Norman MacDonald, born in 1775, and was their father a John MacDonald? (Both Hugh and Norman named their eldest sons John. Traditionally the firstborn was named for his parental grandfather).

Appendix 10

Christianity, Education and the Military

"The People of the Great Faith was the common epithet by which they were mentioned in scorn ...Their fame was spread far and wide as a people ... that ought to be shunned by every one as a pest to society ... These things were grievous to flesh and blood and not easily borne."
Neil Douglas 1797

Rev. D. M. Lamont in his history of the Strath area of Skye, tells us that the earliest religion of the inhabitants of the 'Island' was probably Druidism. This was the religion we associate with the people who erected the first standing stones in various parts of the Western Isles. These early stones, unlike the Pictish stones of Bronze Age times, have no markings. Three Pictish Symbol stones have been found on Skye. They provide evidence that the Picts occupied the island in early times. It is believed that Skye was part of the kingdom of the Picts until 670AD but there is a dispute as to whether the symbols on the stones are Christian or Pagan. All three have the crescent and V-rod symbols but the Tote Stone near Skeabost, also shows a double disc, Z-rod, mirror and comb. Both rods have floriated ends. Of the other two stones, one is at Dunvegan Castle, having been discovered at *Tobar nam Maor* and the third was removed to the Royal Museum in Edinburgh, after recovery from the beach at Fiscavaig.

The earlier times of Druidism probably coincide with the period from which the Fingalian legends come. Traces of this religion lasted long among the Christian Picts and Celts in a diluted form of folk-belief, as witchcraft (*druidheachd*). There were certain places of worship in pre-Christian times involving oak and alder trees which were sacred to the ancient inhabitants. *Lonfearn* (the stream of the alders) in Trotternish was probably one of these, and perhaps there were once alder groves thereabouts. The remains of a number of beehive dwellings are still in evidence. It is thought these were once inhabited by the wise men, priests and judges of the ancient Picts and Celts. The local name for them is *Tighean Druineach* (Druids' Houses). Some commentators also believe that the name of the township of *Achnahanaid* (Field of the Mother Church) in the Braes district, is itself pre-christian and was an ancient centre of Druidism. This old Picto/Celtic religion had Sun Worship at its centre and we have already mentioned some of the 'sun-wise' practices which have lingered in Celtic tradition. Perhaps there is significance in the Druid belief that Heaven (*Flaith Innis*) translates as '**Island** of the Blessed'.

Most commentators agree that Christianity was first brought to the Isle of Skye, from Ireland, by *Saint Columba* around 585 A.D. Having founded the monastery of Iona in 563 A.D., he, and various other Irish monks, among them *Maol Luag*, Bishop of Lismore (Kilmaluag), *Talorgan* (Kiltaraglen) and *Martin* (Kilmartin), came to north Skye, setting up various daughter monasteries to the principal one at Iona. Within Trotternish, in the parishes of Kilmuir, Portree and Snizort there are some thirty remains of places of worship founded by these early monks. (Kil- means chapel or monk's cell). In Portree Bay itself there is a St. Columba Island with its ruined chapel. The significance of many of these religious remains being on small islands lies in the vow of monasticism taken by the monks. *Columba's* declared motive for coming to Scotland was to become an *'exile for Christ'* and much of his time would have been spent in prayer and fasting.

The original name of Portree Bay was *Loch Chaluim Chille* or St. Columba's Loch. Born at Garten, County Donegal, Ireland in 521, *St. Columba* became Abbot of Iona. He belonged to Clan O'Donnell, and was of royal descent. His father's name was *Fedhlimdh* and his mother *Eithne* and he was given the baptismal name *Colum* meaning 'dove', but the manner of his early life meant that he was regarded as *Crimthan* meaning 'wolf'. Later he became known as *Colum-cille*, 'the dove of the churches', with regard to the many which he had set up. He is most closely associated with the north of Skye where all of the little chapels are on islets, either in sea lochs, freshwater lochs or indeed a river.

Although there are several ruined churches or monasteries in north Skye which are named after this saint, there is some evidence to suggest that the one in the Skeabost River was his principal abode while in the island. A large rock, one of the two *Clachan Glasa*, to the right of the old road at Skeabost Hall, is said to be a pulpit from which he preached.

"St Columba's island in the Snizort River just below the bridges in Skeabost, is undoubtedly the most significant historical site in Skye. Its significance lies in the extent to which the rise and fall of this ecclesiastical complex depended on national and international politics."

So wrote Dr Alasdair Maclean, brother of the late poet Dr Sorley Maclean, and **the** expert on the history of this site.

From Norwegian documents of the 11th Century, we learn that it was then the seat of the Bishop of Skye, also called, the Bishop of *Sodor*. (As mentioned earlier, the *Sudereys* were the Southern or Western Isles as opposed to the *Nordereys* Orkney and Shetland.) This Bishopric was subject to the Archdiocese of Trondheim.

The first such Bishop of Skye was *Wymund* or *Hamun*, consecrated in 1079 at York.

Following the Battle of Largs in 1263, Norse influence in Skye began to wane, and by 1266 Skye was liberated from Norse rule after a period of some 400 years. With the departure of the invaders, power came to MacDonald Lord of the Isles. He reigned supreme until 1491 when the Kings of Scotland succeeded in breaking the power chain. The importance of Snizort, under the patronage of the Lords of the Isles, can be seen in the fact that in 1428 Angus MacDonald, son of the chief, and cousin of King James I of Scotland was appointed

Bishop of Snizort. With his father's support he was able to defy papal authority, his father threatening to remove the treasures from the Abbey of Iona. These treasures could well have ended up in Snizort if agreement had not been reached with the Benedictines. St. Columba's continued as the seat of the Bishops of the Isles until 1498, when it was moved to Iona.

The Cathedral at Snizort was a small one; the nave and chancel combined measure only 80feet. It may never have been intended as a permanent one. Bishop William Russel considered that the Isle of Man still lay in his Episcopal jurisdiction, and in 1499 hoped that the Isle of Man would be recovered from England. The present (2010) Anglican Bishopric is styled *Sudor and Man*.

It is said that the Cathedral was vacated in 1695, possibly as a result of erosion of the island by the river.

In the south transept can be seen a high relief of a knight in armour. This slab belonged to the MacSwan, MacSwain or MacSween clan. Outside the north transept there is a damaged slab with a representation of Madonna and Child.

The other building of importance, to the west of the Cathedral proper, is better preserved. Known as Nicolson's Aisle, this is believed to be the burial place of 28 chiefs, or chief men, of Clan Nicolson, Skye's oldest clan. It is probably contemporary with the 11th Century Cathedral, as the Nicolsons are believed to have come to Skye around 950 AD.

Within the Cemetery are also to be found the graves of three generations of MacQueen ministers of Snizort. The Rev. Archibald MacQueen's headstone is believed to be part of an arch from the Cathedral. Donald MacQueen and Donald Munro, noted lay preachers of the 18th century, are also buried here. Donald Munro was known as the blind fiddler and was born at *Achtalean*, near *Achachork* on the outskirts of Portree. He had an enormous influence on the religion of both, those people who emigrated from Skye, and those who remained.

Near the cemetery is the site of the Battle of Trotternish in1528 between the MacDonald and MacLeod clans. The battlefield, on what is now the Skeabost Golf Course, is called *Achadh na Fala*, the Field of Blood. It is said that the severed heads of the corpses were disposed of in the river and collected in a pool still known as *Coire nan Ceann*, the Cauldron of the Heads. This battle, or perhaps it was another in 1539, decided the ownership of Trotternish. Donald Gorm MacDonald defeated the MacLeods. Therafter, the Snizort River became the boundary between MacDonald and MacLeod territories.

Another two Irish monks were of importance in Skye's early religious history. *Kilmaluag*, in Trotternish, was named for the cell or chapel of *St. Moluag*, Bishop of Lismore and a colleague of *St. Columba*, the ruins of which were recently traced nearby. This monk is also associated with a church on Raasay, as well as the *Teampaill Moluaidh* at Ness in the Isle of Lewis.

At *Borline* on *Loch Eynort* there is a very ancient settlement with the remains of two churches. The older and smaller one was dedicated to *St. Maelrubha*, a monk who, like *St. Moluag*, also came from Ulster. *Maelrubha's* main church was on the mainland of Scotland, at Applecross, *A' Chomaraich* (the sanctuary), founded in 673 A.D., and it was here that he died in 722. The old *Borline* church is marked on maps as *Kilmoruy,* a corruption of the saint's name. The carving of an abbot on the high Celtic cross in the churchyard is said to be a portrait of *Maelrubha*, and a stone font, dated 1430, now in the Museum of Antiquities in Edinburgh, may also show a representation of the saint.

In the churchyard are several ancient gravestones which confirm that this was a very important religious site for hundreds of years. It is said that the National Covenant of Scotland (*"to maintain the true religion and the King's majesty"*) was signed here by all the Clan Chiefs and principal men of Skye in 1642. It had originally been drawn up and *"subscribed by the King's Majesty and Household in 1580"* and re-instated by the General Assembly of 1639. It became an Act of Parliament in 1640 requiring signature by all those of *'rank and quality'*, but it took the commissioners a considerable time to get around the whole of Scotland. Of course they arrived at *Loch Eynort* by ship. The later, larger church ruin was probably in use at this time and its minister was Rev. John MacKinnon. The Synod of Argyll were so impressed by his indigence that they decided to confer on him *"twelve bolls of victual out of the vacant parishes of Kintyr"* in order to relieve his immediate wants.

The Celtic Church

Rev. Donald Lamont maintains that there was a long struggle between the old Druidism religion and the new Christianity of the Celtic Church. *"This was not a war of bloodshed but a trial of strength in arguments and miracle-working. The historian Adamnan puts miracles first and preaching second in St. Columba's work....... The people must have spectacular proof that the God of Columba was greater than the gods of their fathers. When he landed in Skye, as he was entering the woods a terrible wild boar of extraordinary size made at him. The saint raised his holy hand to God and said: 'Come no farther in this direction; on the spot to which thou has now come, die.' As the sound of the saint's words rang through the woods, quickly before his very face it fell down and died."*

Was it perhaps at *Tote*, near Skeabost that St Columba slew the wild boar? A rock with a prominent 'hoofmark' is pointed out as the place where the wild creature's charge was brought to a halt when the good man prayed!

The Celtic form of Christian worship continued to make progress in spite of regular raids by the heathen Norsemen or Vikings, who were gradually assimilated into the island communities. In 880 A.D. Harald Haarfager became King of Norway and those opposed to his accession fled from his vengeance and sought to establish themselves in the Hebrides. These Norse invaders are believed to have been wantonly cruel, and particularly so toward religious establishments. In 802 they attacked Iona, massacring 68 monks of the sacred island. Some historians believe that the Norse settlers and the native Celts of Skye lived as separate races in different parts of the island and that the *Duns* and *Borgs* in Skye placenames illustrate this well. Both words 'dun' and 'borg' mean a fort. The *borgs* were in the hands of the Norse and the *duns* under Celtic control, so that places like *Kingsborg* and *Scudaborg* were Viking strongholds while *Dun Torvaig* and *Dun Gerishader* were held by the native tribes. Each *dun* was built within sight of several others so that messages could be passed swiftly across the island. It is believed that the network of *duns,* which can be traced on a map of Skye, was used to warn the natives of further Viking raids. Be that as it may, it is interesting to note that many of Skye's placenames have a Viking origin, particularly coastal features, and yet very few other words from the Norse language have been assimilated into Gaelic. This is believed to have been as a result of very few Norse women venturing to the Hebrides, so that the children of 'mixed marriages' and rapes spoke their 'mother-tongue' rather than the language of their fathers. Thus the Gaelic language and Celtic Christianity predominated in Skye, learned 'at mother's knee'.

In the month of September 1263, the local Braes people might have observed the vast fleet of King *Haakon* of Norway sweeping south under full sail through the *Sound of Raasay* to *Kyleakin* (Kyle Haakon) and thence to utter defeat by Alexander III of Scotland at the Battle of Largs. Haakon's own longboat was of great dimensions, built entirely of oak, and ornamented with richly carved dragons, overlaid with gold which would doubtless have reflected the rays of the autumn sun. He had sailed from Norway in July and had travelled via Lewis and north Skye where he had added greatly to his fleet. More than a hundred galleys sailed past Braes and we know that one of them was commanded by an Andrew Nicolson of *Trotternish.* (As mentioned earlier, Skye's oldest Clan, the Nicolsons, are said to have taken possession of *Scorrybreck* and *Lonfearn* in 950 A.D.)

On their return from the battle, King *Haakon's* fleet sought refuge in Loch Bracadale, *Vestrafjord* or *Wester Fjord*, before sailing north. In Orkney, the king died of his wounds. Three years later, at the Treaty of Perth, *Haakon's* successor, *Magnus*, gave up all claims to the Scottish Isles and Norse rule of the Hebrides came to an end.

The Celtic Church with its bishops, abbots and monasteries, continued to predominate in Scotland until Queen Margaret introduced Romanist practices in 1069, but in remote Highland areas the old church, with few alterations, lingered long after that. Following the Reformation of the 16th century, the religion of Skye was mainly Episcopalian. In Alexander Nicolson's *'History of Skye'*, we read that at the time of the Statutes of Iona, 1608 – 1616, after James VI of Scotland had become James I of England, when the clan chiefs agreed that; *"the pastors to be planted are to be reverently obeyed, their stipends dutifully paid, the ruinous kirks, with reasonable diligence, to be repaired, the Sabbaths solemnly kept, adulteries and such vile slanders to be severely punished......the chiefs to profess the true religion publicly taught within the realm of Scotland, and embraced by His Majesty and his estates, as the only and undoubted truth of God."* 'most, if not all, the ministers of Skye were Episcopalian, although the government supported Presbyterianism.' Throughout the 18th century, Highland Episcopalians, although they continued to pray for the monarch, refused to acknowledge the Houses of Orange or Hanover until there remained no Stuart to claim the throne.

The first Skye minister to; *'dispense the sacrament according to the rites of the Protestant faith'* was the Rev. Neil MacKinnon of Strath. He was at first Episcopalian but later became a Presbyterian. In 1627 he agreed to surrender *'all the Papists of the Isles to the Clerk of the Council'*. It was not until 1642, however, that the Presbytery of Skye is first mentioned, when it was joined by the General Assembly to the Synod of Argyll. Neil MacKinnon submitted a Gaelic translation of the Shorter Catechism to the Synod, which was highly commended as; *"he is a man able in that language."* Many of Skye's ministers became Presbyterians, but at the time of the Restoration in 1660, King Charles II made successful efforts to restore Episcopacy to Skye. In a statement to the Privy Council in 1666, Rev. Donald Nicolson, who was not only minister of Kilmuir but also the chief of the Nicolson clan, avered that; *'there were only six Non-conformists in the whole of Skye'.* By 1689, however, the position was again reversed and only Rev. Nicolson himself, and Rev. Angus MacQueen of Sleat, had refused to take the oath of allegiance to the new rulers, William and Mary. Presbyterianism had now been firmly accepted by those that mattered, the chiefs and clergy.

In the Protestant churches, the Sacrament of the Lord's Supper was dispensed not as the 'trans-substantiated body and blood' of Christ, as in the Roman Mass, but using common bread and wine as 'symbols of His broken body and shed blood'. The institution of twice-yearly Communion Seasons was begun, in which the people of the parish were suitably prepared for the solemnity of the Sacrament. The Thursday was designated a day for 'Confession of sins' or 'spiritual fast day'. Friday was a day for 'Self-examination' and the Saturday a day of 'Preparation and Prayer' for the communicants who would sit at the Lord's Table on the coming Sabbath. On the Monday following, a suitably uplifting concluding sermon was preached. These occasions were attended by large numbers of the common people from neighbouring parishes. It is significant that, although there are a few refererences to Communion Seasons in Highland history books, the best descriptions are from the histories of the Skye emigrants in Canada and Australia. For example, Charles W. Dunn in *'Highland Settler'* has this description. *"For the Presbyterians in the New World the most important religious event of the year was Communion Week, a ceremony imported from Scotland. Communion Week was celebrated wherever there was a Presbyterian church, or even where there was none. Men, women and children gathered from far and near. Some walked twenty, forty, and even fifty miles; walked bare-foot carrying* a pair of shoes in their hands so that their foot-wear would be fresh for the occasion. They slept in the barns and farm-houses of their friends and were fed by them. House-wives in Cape Breton remember serving meals to as many as a hundred visiting celebrants every day during the five-day ceremony.

The event began on Thursday, when the people gathered to humiliate themselves before God. Friday was devoted to the 'ceisd' (question) – a period of absorbing interest to all present. A worthy elder of the congregation presented a text before the gathering, and those who were skilled in theological subtleties – especially other elders of the church – were called upon to demonstrate, in the light of the text, the marks of a true Christian. Many who spoke were not widely read and possessed little formal education, but their knowledge of the Scriptures was profound, and they applied this knowledge in a manner which their descendants, although better schooled, claim they cannot equal. The underlying purpose of the discussion was that those who felt they were making some progress in the difficult task of living a Christian life should provide encouragement and advice to younger or weaker bretheren.

Saturday was dedicated to the spiritual preparation of those who were to receive Communion on the following day. The Sacrament on Sunday was the climax of the Communion Week. No church was large enough to contain the crowds which assembled, and the service was conducted out-of-doors. A tent for the clergy was pitched in a large field near the church; the Communion table, covered with white linen, was set in front of the tent; and benches for the comminicants were arranged in rows on the grass. Here, in the open air, more than a thousand people would congregate to celebrate the Lord's Supper in the traditional manner practised by their forefathers in the Highlands and Islands of Scotland. On Monday a final service of thanksgiving was held, after which the celebrants returned to their homes throughout the countryside."

This description shows how the Highland emigrants had transposed the significant parts of their religious culture to their new homes.

Back in Skye, many of the early Presbyterian ministers, although well educated in both secular and religious matters, lacked spirituality and seemed more concerned with material gain. Alexander Nicolson comments that in the first portion of the 18th century;

> "....some of the clergy lost heart for their work and allowed themselves to sink into the morass of apathy that surrounded them. From being indifferent ministers of the Gospel, they naturally developed into assiduous cultivators of the soil and their good fat glebes soon came to absorb their whole attention."

(The Clan Donald Estate Records for 1833/34 record the Rev. Coll Macdonald of Portree, not only tenanting the glebe lands of *Peinmore* on the east side of the river *Varagill* but also sharing *Tota-Thaoig* and its hill grazing to the west - a rather lucrative second job!)

It had become traditional for the younger sons of the clan chiefs and their important tacksmen to choose between a career in the Church or in the British Army. Often, an appointment to a country parish was regarded as a sinecure for the idle nobility, and dry sermons and prayers were read by the moderate incumbents who had little interest in the spiritual, or temporal, needs of their parishioners. It is interesting to note that almost all of Skye's clergymen during the 18th and early 19th century were of the upper social class and that the clan chiefs and other land proprietors had an important say in which minister was appointed to a parish. The ordinary people, of course, had no say! It would be wrong however, to suggest that none of the ministers had an interest in the spiritual welfare of their flocks; indeed one or two of the clergy were shining examples of their calling.

A tale is told of the first Lord MacDonald, 17th Chief of the Clan, and proprietor of Trotternish. On one occasion, while residing in his hunting lodge above Portree Bay, one of several throughout the island, he worshiped in the Portree Parish Church. The minister was Rev. John Nicolson, himself the son of the tacksman of Scorrybreck. Following the service, the noble Lord enquired why the preacher had not, as was the custom, made a specific petition for his Lordship and family in his prayers. The minister replied; *"Indeed I did pray for you, and yours, in my petition for the Lord to have mercy on **all** sinners."*

In the Old Statistical Account it is said of John Nicolson; *"a man of primitive letters and exemplary life; sincere, benevolent and charitable, of untainted rectitude and uprightness, and of such indefatigable perserverance in the discharge of his pastoral office, that being appointed to preach in Kirktown in Raasay once every month and once a quarter in another part of the island, of no easy access, he has not been absent above four times on the ordinary days during the whole course of his ministry."*

This minister, *"of powerful personality and striking appearance"*, died in the last year of the 18th century and was succeeded by Rev. Alexander Campbell, son of the tacksman of *Corlarach*. He had been both schoolmaster and catechist in Portree since 1791.

It was not however, through the agency of ministers that Skye was to experience religious revival in the 19th century, but the Holy Spirit was pleased to work first through catechists and schoolmasters, educating the people and explaining the Gospel in their native language.

In 1686 two hundred copies of the Bible translated into Irish Gaelic had been sent to Protestant ministers in the Highlands, for the use of their parishioners; and in 1767 the New Testament had been translated into Scottish Gaelic, but few of the common people could read. Some members of the Scottish Society for the Propagation of Christian Knowledge (SSPCK), a body which had done much in setting up schools in the Highlands, actually opposed the provision of the whole of the Bible in Gaelic on the grounds that it would tend to preserve the distinction between Lowlander and Highlander. The Society wished to promote English as the only language through the medium of which the people ought to be educated. Even the quintessential Englishman Samuel Johnson could see the flaw in this argument. *"I did not expect to hear that it could be, in an assembly convened for the propagation of Christian knowledge, a question whether any nation instructed in religion should receive instruction; or whether that instruction should be imparted to them by a translation of the holy books into their own language ...... To omit the most efficacious method of advancing Christianity is a crime of which I know not that the world has yet an example."*

It is very sad that some of the Established Church leaders, even as late as 1824, had a marked bias against the Gaelic language. In that year Rev. Norman MacLeod attempted to encourage the Church of Scotland to print a quarto volume of the Bible in large clear print, as the commonest available version could only be read by the young and clear-sighted. The reply he received was *"Just advise your Highland friends to get spectacles."*

Comments like these seem completely at odds with the determination of the Protestant leaders of the 16th century to outlaw the Latin Mass and to teach the people in the language of the common people. In Skye, at this time, the language of the common people was Gaelic!

The approved version of the Gaelic Shorter Catechism published in 1651 was distributed widely with a strong recommendation that it be committed to memory. Schoolmasters were encouraged to teach it to their pupils and, as soon as the latter had acquired a reasonable proficiency in the reading of it, they were to go from house to house and teach those of their neighbours who could not themselves read the Catechism in Gaelic.

It is sometimes difficult for commentators and historians to remain objective, particularly with regard to matters of religion.

Their own faith, or absence of faith, is bound to colour their arguments and this is doubtless true in the cases of many that I quote here. It is also, no doubt, true in my own case.

One Skye historian, writing about the beginning of the 19th century, tells us that there was much confusion among pastors and people as to what constitured true Christian religion: *"Druidism, Romanism and Protestantism, each contributed an element of the grotesque superstition that went under the name of religion. The island was peopled by witches, fairies, and ghosts: darkness covered the land and gross darkness the people. Drunken and riotous excesses abounded. These were practised in connection with the most sacred events. At funerals great quantities of ardent spirits were consumed before lifting the body. The most outrageous orgies were indulged in: bagpipes were played, songs sung, filthy tales and jests recounted."*

How very surprising then, that by 1841, the comments made about the morality of Skye people are so different.

Rev. A. Clark; *"The people are generally remarkably sober. Their hospitality continues as unbounded as ever; but in the exercise of it, the rules of temperance and decorum are very rarely violated, and every excess is condemned and discouraged."*

Rev. Coll MacDonald; *"The vices of profane swearing and drunkenness are less prevalent than they were twenty years ago. The people are powerfully under the influence of moral principles, so much so that heinous crimes are seldom or ever seen or heard of among them."*

Was this remarkable transformation brought about as a result of the restraining influence of the large numbers of the population who were converted in the Skye Revivals?

On the outskirts of Portree, between *Achachork* and *Drumuie*, once stood the now long-abandoned township of *Achtalean*. There are many such deserted villages in Trotternish as a result of emigration and clearance, but this one is remembered as the birthplace of one of the island's most influential sons. Donald Munro was born here in 1773, becoming an excellent exponent of the highland fiddle. At the age of fourteen he contacted smallpox which left him blind. Munro was a popular entertainer and travelled a great deal around north Skye. On one occasion in 1805, at an open-air meeting in *Uig*, he came in contact with John Farquharson, an evangelist from Glen Tilt in Perthshire, whose ship, on passage to America, had become stormbound in the sheltered bay. Farquharson was described by Principal Daniel Dewar of Marischal College, Aberdeen as *"the most wonderful man I have ever known, Divine power accompanied his ministry."* It was surely this Divine power which led to the conversion of the blind fiddler who became the "Father of Evangelical Religion" in Skye, and, not without significance, that the text on which the preacher spoke was, *'I am the door; by me if any man enter in he shall be saved, and shall go in and out and find pasture'*, as the doors of the Established Church had been shut to the large gathering!

The doors of the National Church, in several parts of Skye, remained closed to Donald Munro and those who espoused his revivalist doctrine, but the ordinary people of Skye had an open heart for this popular preacher and, like his Lord and Master, it was said that *"the common people heard him gladly"*. He was led by the hand from place to place, and there were those even prepared to carry him on their backs if need be. Following the revival of 1812 to 1814, during which very large numbers of people, of all ages, were converted, it appears to have been universally acknowledged, even by the opposing clergy, that the effects on the island were extremely positive. In later years, many writers have commented disparagingly on Munro for having had an adverse effect on the traditional music of Skye, as he had burned his own fiddle when he found a greater joy, and encouraged others to do likewise.

Many of Donald Munro's converts continued his good work throughout the island catechising and educating the people. It was later that evangelical ministers began to stir themselves. The best known of these was Rev. Roderick MacLeod, *Maighstir Ruaraidh*, who was a student in Aberdeen at the time of

Farquharson's visit to Skye. He was the son of the moderate Parish Minister of Snizort, Rev. Malcolm MacLeod.

Rev. Roderick, while still an ordained missionary at *Lynedale*, visited Rev. John Shaw in the *Bracadale Manse*. Here he saw a copy of Bellamy's 'Christian Religion Delineated' and Chalmers' 'Lectures on Romans' on Shaw's bookshelf. Having read these he became concerned about his own spiritual condition. The resulting change in his life and preaching soon became apparent to many of his clerical associates who *"often spoke with bitterness about evangelical religion"*. Shortly after Rev. Shaw died, *Maighstir Ruaraidh* was presented to the *Bracadale* parish by Chief MacLeod of MacLeod. He later claimed that his appointment here was on account of his lineage and of his ability *"as a good shot"*, which appealed to the landowning aristocracy, rather than his godliness or preaching ability. It was at open-air meetings at *Fairy Bridge* in the 1840s that evidence developed of a further religious revival. Huge numbers flocked from all over Skye to listen to the preaching of Rev Roderick MacLeod. Indeed a church here would have been superfluous, as the numbers that gathered could be measured in thousands rather than hundreds. An eye witness in 1842 said; *"I saw the young and old, male and female, pouring forth from all sides of the land, from hills, and valleys, villages, hamlets and lonely huts. The loch too was covered with about fifty skiffs, like the multitudes which dotted the sea of Tiberias, in pursuit of the Lord himself when He was manifest in the flesh."*

Nowadays it is hard to believe the distances that people of all ages were prepared to walk to these services. No doubt there were shortcuts through the hills and there would be good company, but to walk to *Fairy Bridge* from *Braes, Glenmore* and *Portree*, which many did, is truly astonishing.

Maighstir Ruaraidh's support of the Free Church, which became popular with 'ordinary' people at the Disruption of 1843, led to a backlash from some landowners who supported the 'Established Church', over which they continued to have some influence through patronage. In 1846 at least 16 families

in his new Snizort congregation were ejected from their holdings. In 1847 a further 30 families received notices to quit. This
evidence was given to a House of Commons Select Committee
on 12th May 1847. Although many of those evicted were the
sub-tenants of tacksmen or 'gentlemen farmers' in the parish, all
were, directly or indirectly, the responsibility of the clan chiefs,
who remained the proprietors of the estates. Whether or not the
clan chief or only his factor had signed the orders is immaterial.

The first Free Church Minister of Bracadale, Rev. John
Finlayson, had to fulfil his pastoral duties for a year, by walking
to and from Portree, a distance of 24 miles, as he was refused
accommodation in the parish!

Many of the ministers of the Established Church, through
patronage, owed their appointments to the landowners, and
tended to take the side of *"the powers that be which are ordained
of God"*, while encouraging the people to submit to the whims
of their superiors and betters. The Rev. Roderick MacLeod was
appointed moderator of the Free Church in 1863. In his moder-
atorial address, he referred to the outstanding contribution
made by Skyemen to the British Army and Empire in the period
before 1815.

> *"The men of Skye were of more value in those days. Times have
> changed. The cry is now, 'Away with them, away with them!'
> Sheep, it appears, are more worthy of keeping."*

Only after many years of open-air services, were the inhabitants of Trotternish eventually granted permission and land on
which to build Free Churches. Dr. Sorley MacLean however
comments that: *"By the time of the crofter resurgence in the 1880s,
the Free Church had, to a certain extent, itself become a church of the
Establishment."*

For residents of Camustianavaig, the parish church was four
miles away in Portree and so could only be attended on special

occasions. There was a church at Ollach, the central Braes township, from the early 1800s and, as this was only a mile and a half distant, and usually supplied by a very competent, Gaelic-speaking, lay-preacher or missionary such as Walter MacKay, Angus MacNeil, Nicol Nicolson, Donald MacQueen or Donald MacDonald, it was the venue of choice on the Lord's Day. (These were some of the 'Men of Skye' mentioned in Roderick MacCowan's book, as preachers in Braes.)

We understand that a new Braes Free church was erected, in 1878 by the architect James Mattews, on the Ollach site and it was this church that became famous for the first meeting, in the spring of 1883, of the Napier Commission to examine the treatment of crofting tenants. The first spokesman, Angus Stewart of Peinachoran, set the tone with his succinct analysis of the problem, and its solution;

> *"I cannot bear evidence to the distress of my people without bearing evidence to the oppression and high-handedness of the landlord and his factor.....The smallness of our holdings and the inferior quality of the land is what has caused our poverty; and the way in which the poor crofters are huddled together, and the best part of the land devoted to deer forests and big farms.....What would remedy the people's grievances throughout the island of Skye is to give them plenty of land, as there is plenty of it, and they are willing to work it. Give us the land out of the plenty of land that is about for cultivation.*
>
> *That is the principal remedy that I see - give us the land!"*

One of the results of these religious revivals was seen in the relish that many of the ordinary folk of Skye had for God's Word and Ordinances, although their personal lives were beset by so many severe domestic difficulties.

Lewellin's advice to potential emigrants to PEI was unnecessary, as far as Skye settlers were concerned. They would certainly not go without their Gaelic Bibles!

"Don't forget to put up your Bible, with any other good books, and school-books for your children, if you have a family. Education is now estimated at something like its value. The Legislature have shewn a laudable desire to promote it. May they never cease their efforts on this interesting subject, until the holy wish of our late pious Monarch George III, shall be accomplished, as it regards this Colony—his philanthropic and christian wish that 'every child in his dominions should be able to read the Bible.'".

Education

"Education has always had a high place in Scotland. Even before the Reformation there were four universities in Scotland but only two in England. Knox's famous idea was to have a school in every parish, a high school in every major town and the opportunity given even to the poorest student to go to university. The Book of Discipline of which he was the author proposed that the wealth of the pre-Reformation church be divided between the maintenance of the ministry, education for all and the care of the poor. Sadly the greedy nobility refused to pass The Book of Discipline in Parliament and devised means to acquire the revenue of the church lands for themselves. Nevertheless, the Reformation emphasis on education did bear fruit. Even in 1830 the English Universities had less than 3000 students whereas the Scottish ones had 4400 students. Yet England's population was eight times that of Scotland."

Rev. William MacLeod, former Free Church Minister Portree (2009)

I am obliged to my former teacher and colleague Mr Alister Ross for the following information about Skye schools.

'The earliest known school in Skye was the grammar school founded in 1651 at *Duntulm* by clan chief Sir James Mòr Macdonald. Later in the same century, the first school known to have existed in Portree was established in 1697 – one year after the Scottish Parliamentary Act of 1696, the "Act for Settling of

Schools". The school, at Kiltaraglen, was founded by Sir Donald Macdonald of Sleat, the grandson of Sir James Mòr, and its purpose was to educate boys of the upper classes only.

Indeed, the more comprehensive Reformation idea of a school in every parish was slow to develop: according to the Old Statistical Account of 1795, there were schools in only three of the Skye parishes – Portree, Sleat and Strath. This deficiency led to much voluntary and private effort in the course of the eighteenth and nineteenth centuries. For example, by 1822 the Scottish Society for Propagating Christian Knowledge had six schools in Skye. For a long time these schools refused to use Gaelic as a medium of instruction, and consequently made little impact.

In 1763, a school for "higher education" – that is, to prepare pupils for university – was set up in Portree. It attracted pupils from throughout Skye and from the mainland, but was discontinued in 1825 because of the difficulty of finding a suitably qualified school master. (**The fact that Alexander MacLeod, brother of our Murdoch, was regarded as the 'Father of Education' in Lot 67 PEI, speaks volumes for the quality of teaching he benefited from at Portree School!**)

The first parish school in Portree, though, was established early in the nineteenth century. It was situated in the building which was then the westernmost house in Wentworth Street, on the site of what is now the Caledonian Hotel. The first schoolmaster of whom any record exists was Murdo Macdonald, a Ross-shire man, who became known as "The Old Schoolmaster". Having attended university for two sessions, Murdo Macdonald taught for twenty-three years before his professional attainments, experience and skill were recognised on the 2nd of July 1848 in a diploma granted by the Educational Institute of Scotland.

In 1822, there were 36 schools in Skye, but by 1837 this number had dropped to 31, before rising again to 35 in 1840. By the mid-nineteenth century the population was increasing, with the introduction of vaccination resulting in a drop in infant mortality rates. The Skye population in 1841 was 23,074 – more than double the figure of 1755.

The Second Statistical Account of 1841 refers to four schools in the parish of Portree. Of these, two were Gaelic schools, and the other two parochial schools – one run by a society based in Glasgow. In the parochial schools, one of which would be in the village itself, the subjects taught were English, reading, writing, grammar, arithmetic, book-keeping, geography, Latin and elements of Greek. A Branch School of the Portree Parochial School was set up in Raasay, which taught only the elementary branches. Only the children living in the immediate vicinity of the schools would attend them.

One of the Gaelic schools would probably likewise be in the village, and one of them seems to have been financed and controlled by The Gaelic School Society, which had been founded in 1811 to promote Bible education in the Highlands. Between 1843 and 1846, this society came under the control of the Free Church. It may be safe to assume that the old Gaelic school, which must have existed from the early years of the nineteenth century, developed into the Free Church School in the single-storey thatched building on the Meall, to the east and adjoining the churchyard. (Later on, this building was occupied by John Macrae, a fisherman, and it was eventually demolished by order of the County Council.) The schoolmaster of the Free Church School for some time was a John Finlayson.'

The SSPCK (The Scottish Society for the Propagation of Christian Knowledge) was formed by Royal Charter in 1709 for the purpose of founding schools *"where religion and virtue might be taught to young and old"* in the Scottish Highlands and other *"uncivilised areas of the country"*. Their schools were a valuable addition to the Church of Scotland programme of education in Scotland, which was already working with support from a tax on landowners to provide a school in every parish. The SSPCK had 5 schools by 1711, 25 by 1715, 176 by 1758 and 189 by 1808 with 13,000 pupils attending. Sadly the

SSPCK avoided using Gaelic as the medium of instruction with the result that pupils learned by rote without understanding what they read. In 1741 the SSPCK introduced a Gaelic-English vocabulary. Then in 1767 it brought in a New Testament with facing pages of Gaelic and English texts. It was however the Gaelic School Society GSS that began to promote Gaelic as the medium of instruction in areas where Gaelic was the native tongue.

"The voluntary Gaelic School Society was founded in Edinburgh in 1811 with the object of teaching the people of the Highlands and Islands to read the Scriptures in Gaelic, their mother tongue.

These schools were built and maintained by the community and were of simple construction. The walls were of undressed natural stone with a thatched roof. They were sparsely furnished with home made stools, and the lighting and heating was poor. Teachers were appointed for their Godliness rather than their academic qualifications. They were referred to as 'Sgoilean Chrìosd', the Schools of Christ, and these buildings became the forerunners of the more sophisticated village Prayer Houses.

In some places these schools were called 'Tighean Leughadh', Reading Houses, or 'Tighean Sgoil', School Houses. The walls of the original Gaelic Schools in many places may still be seen.

The Gaelic Teachers Guidebook stated that a Sabbath School for the children was to be held in the forenoon and on the Sabbath afternoons there was to be a one-hour session of instruction for adults. On the Sabbath evening after 6pm a Prayer Meeting was to be held in the school building for the benefit of all who attended. In that way the institution of the village Sunday School as well as the village midweek and Sunday evening Prayer Meetings were first introduced by The Gaelic Society.

The New Testament first appeared in Gaelic in 1767, but the whole Bible was not translated into Gaelic until 1801, yet it was a closed book to the people of the islands because they could not read Gaelic or English. It is said that the Scriptures

were not available in some of the islands, in the people's
language until the 1820s.

It was through the medium of Gaelic instruction that real
progress was achieved in educating the people of Skye, and that
was through voluntary organisations.

There was a magnificent response to the opportunity for the
first time to read the Scriptures in their own tongue. Adults as
well as children attended the Gaelic Schools and the treasure
house of the Scriptures soon influenced the minds and outlook
of the people, and dispelled the superstitions in which the
people lived. In that way the manners and culture of the people
were improved. We owe a great deal to these simple Gaelic
Schools.

The Gaelic Society Schools were circulatory, which meant
that they moved from place to place, usually every three years,
but the period varied and every village, however small, would
have a school for at least a year."

From The "Angus MacLeod Archive", Kershader, Isle of
Lewis.

The expansion of these Societies was only possible by
generous and sometimes large donations of capital. They were
also prepared to adapt to the needs of the population. In the
second charter by George II of 1738, the SSPCK was empow-
ered over and above the purposes of the original patent *"to
instruct pupils in husbandry, housewifery, trading, manufacturing or
manual occupations"*.

One of the stipulations of the GSS was that *'the teachers to
be employed by the Society shall neither be Preachers nor
Public Exhorters, stated or occasional, of any denomination
whatever'*. Steve Taylor comments that *"This was a rule that was
to be bent, broken and cause great problems from the outset."*

Parish ministers in Skye were constantly complaining to the
Society officials that their local teachers were discouraging the
populace from attendance at the parish church and addressing
the people themselves. Of course there was often good reason

for this. Parishes were large so there were long walks to church and, in many cases, the schoolmasters were superior preachers to the sedentary pastors.

The Education Act of 1872 abolished the old management of parish schools and introduced the school board system, which transferred the responsibility of education to the state. Unfortunately this act failed to address the role of Gaelic in education. Even in the first quarter of the 20th century, pupils were punished for speaking Gaelic in the classroom, and in the playground. Fellow scholars were encouraged to report infringements to the schoolmaster! Divide and rule!

The new schools did not meet with favour from Walter MacKay, for 42 years a Gaelic school teacher and lay-preacher in Skye. He began teaching a Sabbath School in Braes in his latter years, stating that; *"The instillation of sound Scriptural Doctrine will serve as an antidote to the infidel instruction the children receive in the Board Schools."*

Military Service

"At the close of the last and at the beginning of the present century (19th), half the farms of Skye were rented by half-pay officers. The Army List was to the Island what the Post Office Directory is to London."

Alexander Smith 'Summer in Skye'

As we have observed previously, after the failure of the Jacobite Risings, the younger sons of the clan chiefs and prominent tacksmen were encouraged to follow a military career in the British Army. These men, as officers, recruited many of their former clansmen to join the Scottish regiments. This life was, of course, seen as a great adventure as well as another possible means of escaping the hardships and difficulties of life in the post-Culloden Highlands. Warfare was in their blood and they were hardened to the rigorous life they were required to lead in many parts of the world.

In the light of Rev. Roderick MacLeod's comments on the value of the men of Skye as soldiers, the numbers can be put into context from a statement made by Rev. Dr. Norman MacLeod known as *Caraid nan Gaidheal* (the Highlander's friend).

> *"From about 1797 to 1837 it is computed that 10,000 private soldiers, 600 commissioned officers under the rank of Colonel, 21 lieutenant-generals and major-generals, 45 colonels and 120 pipers went from Skye to the British army. In that time Skye gave 4 Governors of British colonies, 1 Governor General of India, 1 Adjutant-General of the British Army. At the Battle of Waterloo 1,600 Skyemen fought in the British ranks."*

Prime Minister William Pitt, afterwards Earl of Chatham, in addressing the House of Commons, commented about the Highlanders. *"I have sought for merit wherever it could be found. It is my boast that I was the first minister who looked for it, and found it in the mountains of the north. I called it forth, and drew into your service a hardy and intrepid race of men; men who, when left by your jealousy, became a prey to the artifices of your enemies, and had gone nigh to have overturned the State in the war before last (1745). These men in the last war were brought to combat on your side; they served with fidelity, as they fought with valour in every quarter of the globe."*

Another of those who knew the value of the Highland soldier was General Wolfe who famously conquered Quebec. Having fought at Culloden as an officer in the Duke of Cumberland's army, and having played his part in the Government's barbaric policy of subduing the Highland population, when asked; *"Where can the British Army find more troops?"* The hero replied. *"The Highlands; they are a hardy, intrepid race; and no great mischief if they fall."*

This statement speaks volumes about the attitude of the British Establishment to the **people** of the Highlands of Scotland, and helps us to understand the lack of real interest that successive governments have taken in their welfare.

The Highland geographical area however has interested, and continues to interest, those who would like to exploit it.

Derek Cooper's entry in his gazetteer in this connection is worth quoting.

"Around the middle of the nineteenth century a new industry hit the Highlands and spilled over into the Islands. Large fat men from the Midlands paid even larger and fatter sums of money to be allowed to slaughter anything which could be coaxed and beaten within gun range." By 1885, the shooting rents for some Skye estates were netting more than £1000 per year for the proprietors.

As might be expected, given the fighting spirit of the Highlander, Prince Edward Islanders were only too pleased to support the cause of freedom in World Wars I and II and many fell beside their Skye relatives on the battlefields of Europe and North Africa.

Mike Kennedy, writing in the 'West Highland Free Press' on the occasion of the centenary of the sailing of the 'Polly' from Skye to PEI, says;

"Among the PEI veterans of WW11 was a young man Angus J. MacLean who survived heroic exploits with bomber command and the Dutch resistance to become Premier of PEI and one of the Island's most respected political figures. His rediscovered cousins from Skye and Raasay, Calum, Sorley and Alasdair MacLean, equally distinguished for their work in folklore, literature, history and community service, proved the adage that the apple does not fall far from the tree – even if it grows an ocean away."

Bibliography

Ansdell D.	The People of the Great Faith	1998	Stornoway
Bassin E.	The Old Songs of Skye: Frances Tolmie & Her Circle	1977	London
Bitterman R.& McCallumM	Lady Landlords of Prince Edward Island	2008	Quebec
Blanchard W.	Abegweit Review	1995	Charlotte-town
Boswell J.	The Journal of a Tour to the Hebrides	1786	London
Cameron A.	The History and Traditions of The Isle of Skye	1871	Inverness
Campey L. H.	An Unstoppable Force	2008	Toronto
Campey L. H.	"A Very Fine Class of Immigrants"	2001	Toronto
Cooper D.	Skye	1970	London
Craig D.	On the Crofters' Trail	1990	London
Creighton D.	The Story of Canada	1959	London
Dunn C. W.	Highland Settler	1991	Cape Breton
Gordon S.	The Charm of Skye : The Winged Isle	1929	London
Grant I. F.	Highland Folk Ways	1961	London
Humble B.H.	The Songs of Skye : An Anthology	1934	Stirling
Hunter J.	Scottish Exodus: Travel among a worldwide clan	2005	Edinburgh
Hunter J. & MacLean C.	Skye: The Island	1986	Edinburgh
Johnson S.	A Journey to the Western Isles of Scotland	1774	London

Lamont Rev. D.	Strath in the Isle of Skye	1913	Glasgow
MacColl A.W.	Land, Faith & The Crofting Community	2006	Edinburgh
MacCulloch J.A.	The Misty Isle of Skye	1905	Edinburgh
Macdonald I. G.	On Wings of Skye	2009	Guildford
Macdonald I. G.	Like a Bird on the Wing	2008	Guildford
MacDonald J.	Discovering Skye	1982	Duntulm
MacDonald J.	Flora Macdonald: Heroine of the Jacobite Cause	1989	Duntulm
MacDonald J.	A Short History of Crofting in Skye	1998	Duntulm
MacDonald M.	PEI Women Past and Present		
MacDonell M.	Bards of the Polly		
MacGregor A.A.	Over the Sea to Skye	1926	Edinburgh
MacGregor J.	In the Footsteps of Bonnie Prince Charlie	1988	London
MacKay D.	Scotland Farewell	2006	Edinburgh
MacKenzie W.	Old Skye Tales : Traditions, Reflections and Memories	1933	Culnacnoc
MacLean S.	From Wood to Ridge	1999	Edinburgh
MacLeod B.	Seventeenth Century Skye	1950	Inverness
MacLeod C.	The Cruel Clearance of Raasay	2007	Dunfermline
MacLeod H. S.	The Lamonts of Lyndale	2002	Charlottetown
MacLeod H. S.	The MacLeods of Prince Edward Island	1986	Charlottetown
MacLeod J.	Banner in the West	2008	Edinburgh

MacLeod J.	No Great Mischief If You Fall	1993	Edinburgh
MacLeod J. M.	History of Presbyterianism in Prince Edwaed Island	1904	Chicago
MacNeil J. N.	Tales Until Dawn	2005	Edinburgh
MacPherson F.	Watchman Against the World	1993	Cape Breton
MacPherson G. W.	Highland Myths and Legends	2001	Edinburgh
MacPherson J.	Tales of Ossian	1822	Edinburgh
MacQueen M. A.	Skye Pioneers and "The Island"	1929	Winnipeg
MacSween A.	Skye	1990	Edinburgh
MacSween M. D.	Transhumance in North Skye		
Martin Martin	A Description of the Western Isles of Scotland	1703	London
Meek D.	Mairi Mhor nan Oran	1997	Glasgow
Monro Sir D.	Description of the W. Isles of Scotland called Hybrides	1774	Edinburgh
Newton N.	Skye	1975	Newton Abbot
Nicolson A.	History of Skye (Revised 1994)	1995	Portree
Nicolson A.	Verses by Alexander Nicolson	1893	Edinburgh
Paterson R. C.	The Lords of the Isles. A History of Clan Donald	2008	Edinburgh
Pennant T.	A Tour in Scotland and Voyage to the Hebrides	1774	Chester
Richards E	The Highland Clearances / Scots in Australia	2002	Edinburgh

Sellar W.D.H.& MacLean	The Highland Clan MacNeacail (MacNicol)	1999	Waternish
Sharpe R	Raasay - A Study in Island History	1978	London
Sillar F. C. & Meyler R.	Skye (Islands Series)	1973	Newton Abbot
Smith A.	A Summer in Skye	1865	London
Swire O. F.	Skye: The Island and its Legends	1952	Glasgow
Taylor L.S.	These Quiet Stones	1985	Broadford
Taylor S.	The Skye Revivals	2003	Chichester
Thomson D. S.	The Companion to Gaelic Scotland	1994	Glasgow
Willis D.	The Story of Crofting in Scotland	1991	Edinburgh

Lightning Source UK Ltd.
Milton Keynes UK
UKOW040726230413

209611UK00001B/9/P